TALIBAN'S RETURN: PAKISTAN'S STRATEGIC CROSS ROADS

RAJA FURQAN AHMED

Printed: January, 2024
Edition: 1st
ISBN: 978-969-749-271-8
Price: Rs 1799 PKR, $15 US

www.auraqpublications.com | raabta@auraqpublications.com
@AuraqPublications | @AuraqBooks | +92-300-0571-530
Printed and Bound by ***Passive Printers*** - www.passiveprinters.com

DEDICATED TO

To Almighty Allah and the Holy Prophet Muhmmad (P.B.U.H)

&

LOVING FAMILY

ACKNOWLEDGMENTS

Throughout the writing of this book, I have received great support and assistance from my parents, brother Dr Aqib Raja, friends and my teachers.

ABSTRACT

Pakistan has been facing many challenges and opportunities since the Taliban's re-emergence in Afghanistan in August 2021. In the wake of the Taliban's takeover of Afghanistan's government once again, this book examines the complex dynamics between the two adjacent nations. The critical question also arises, "Why did security threats increase after the re-emergence of the Afghan Taliban?".

The Taliban's return to power in Kabul following the withdrawal of US led NATO troops has presented Islamabad with numerous challenges. First and foremost, Pakistan's security threats have increased on the western border. Cross-border militancy, refugee migration and the flow of criminals are a few important challenges. Secondly, Pakistan's long history with the Afghan Taliban itself poses both obstacles and opportunities. While Pakistan has previously been accused of backing the Taliban, it now has job to handle them. It is a complex effort to balance national interests while fostering a peaceful and stable Afghanistan.

The re-emergence of Taliban has also created socio-economic opportunities for Pakistan. Besides, it enables Pakistan to contribute positively to the promotion of stability and peace in the region and enhance regional economic connectivity.

CONTENTS

INTRODUCTION

The announcement by the United States to pull out its troops from Afghanistan and serious engagement with Afghan Taliban representatives in Doha, Qatar, at the start of 2021 increased the latter offensive to take the maximum area under its control across Afghanistan. Taliban encountered no resistance from the Afghan Army or NATO troops. Hence, it was obvious that after the withdrawal of the US troops from country, the Taliban will come into power but no one was expecting that on August 15, 2021, the group will arrive at the gates of Kabul before complete withdrawal of foreign troops. Immediately, the group declared the "Islamic Emirate of Afghanistan",[1] marking a nail in the coffin of the US-backed Ashraf Ghani's government.

Pakistan as the neighbouring state welcomed the re-emergence of the Afghan Taliban. Pakistan believed that several interests would be accomplished with the re-emergence of Taliban including decreasing role of India in Afghanistan. However, at the same time, some believe that violent terrorist activities will be increased which is creating serious questions for Pakistan.

Pakistan shares Afghanistan's longest border approximately 2,640 kilometres (1,640 miles). Both neighbouring countries also share the same traditions, culture and religion, especially the tribal region which is very connected with Afghan culture and tradition. The border has historically been a hotspot of violence and tension as well as a vital transit route for individuals and

---

[1] "Taliban announce creation of Islamic Emirate of Afghanistan, will rule country through council," *DAWN,* August 19, 2021 https://www.dawn.com/news/1641540

goods going between the two nations.

While formulating the Afghan policy, Islamabad remained inclined towards the Taliban. Pakistan's relationship with the Taliban dates to the mid-1990s and remain continued after the Taliban regime was overthrown by the US-led intervention in 2001. The top leadership of the Taliban moved to Pakistan and controlled the organization from Pakistan. Later on, after US pressure, Pakistan arrested several Taliban leaders including Mullah Abdul Ghani Baradar, also known as Mullah Baradar, who was a co-founder of the Taliban movement.

After the US announced to hold talks with the Taliban, Pakistan played a crucial role in the peace process. Afghan Taliban set up a political office in Doha, Qatar in 2013 at the request of the US to facilitate talks and Pakistan also facilitate both parties. Pakistan's communication with the Afghan Taliban led to the Doha agreement between the US and the insurgent group in February 2020.

The accord might not have been reached without Pakistan's involvement and cooperation. Pakistan was able to bridge the gap between opposing parties and offered a vital connection between the factions. Pakistan was also a significant political player in the area as well and its presence gave the situation a feeling of stability. Pakistan made sure that all parties agreed to a peaceful conclusion during the diplomatic conflict, which was not very simple but both US and Taliban were able to sign the agreement after hard diplomacy, protracted talks and strenuous mediation efforts by Pakistan.

After the fall of Kabul, the majority of Pakistanis[2] were

---

[2] "55 percent Pakistanis 'happy' with Taliban takeover of Afghanistan — survey," *Arab News*, September 14, 2021 https://www.arabnews.pk/node/1928561/pakistan

supporting the Taliban and expected that some sort of peace will become in the region but others believe that Afghanistan's new government is more of a burden than a benefit. Working with Afghanistan's new government has both benefits and challenges for Pakistan. The biggest challenge for Islamabad after Taliban came in power is the increase in militant activities. Militant groups such as Tehreek-e-Taliban Pakistan (TTP), Islamic State Khorasan Province (ISKP) as well as other Baloch militant groups see Taliban victory as motivation for them. Pakistan has recorded 51 per cent increase in terrorist attacks in a single year since the Afghan Taliban seized power in August 2021.[3]

While Pakistan also has a number of advantages, building land corridors through Afghanistan will give Central Asian nations access to Islamabad. Pakistan would be able to access new markets for its goods and strengthen ties with its Muslim-majority countries. Regional connectivity will also benefit Afghanistan's fragile economy. Regional connectivity and collaboration might be boosted due to Kabul's strategic location at the crossroads of Central and South Asia. Cooperation and integration in the area might be advanced by working with the new Afghan administration but it is no secret that Afghanistan has had internal political turmoil in the past and any instability there might have negative impacts on relations.

A stable and peaceful Afghanistan will probably result in better relations between the two nations and would even open up new economic opportunities for Pakistan through increasing commerce and investment. Afghanistan's strong and efficient administration will be

---

[3] "Terror attacks in Pakistan surge by 51pc after Afghan Taliban victory." *DAWN*, October 20, 2022 https://www.dawn.com/news/1715927

able to deal with problems like terrorism and the illicit drug trade. Afghanistan is a landlocked nation with little access to the world's marketplaces. Working with the new administration in Afghanistan might help Pakistan expand its trade and economic prospects, particularly in sectors like agriculture, transportation and energy.

Afghanistan has the chance to collaborate with Pakistani initiatives like the China-Pakistan Economic Corridor (CPEC). The CPEC does not include Afghanistan. However, Afghanistan has shown a desire to participate in the Belt and Road Initiative (BRI), a bigger economic development initiative that also includes CPEC. Building infrastructure including roads, railroads and ports is one of BRI's key goals to promote economic growth in nations that were formerly connected by the old Silk Road. Although the final decision on whether to include Afghanistan in the project lies with the Chinese government, it is likely that Afghanistan might benefit from taking part in the BRI.

The Taliban's dominance in Afghanistan has given Pakistan a geopolitical edge. Pakistan can also act as a bridge between the group and the international community and also peacefull and stable Afghanistan can lead towards a new economic corridor which will benefit south Asian and central Asian nations.

CHAPTER 01

HISTORICAL BACKGROUND

1.1 PAKISTAN - AFGHANISTAN RELATIONS: 1947 TO 1989

Pakistan and Afghanistan share a long but complicated history with deep cultural and social ties as well as conflicts, disagreements and disputes. Pakistan, at its birth in 1947, harboured feelings of more insecurity when compared to India. The Eastern neighbour was already hostile while the western neighbour Afghanistan was not ready to accept Pakistan. The only nation to vote against Pakistan's admission to the UN in 1947 was Afghanistan. The Durand line, which the British drew in 1893 as the two countries' official border, is the main grievance Afghanistan had with Pakistan.[4] Besides making territorial claims on Pakistani territory in the provinces of Khyber Pakhtunkhwa (KP), once known as the North-West Frontier Province (NWFP) and Balochistan, Additionally, Afghanistan provided financial support to the tribal people of Pakistan and encouraged them to challenge the authorities.[5] The Afghan representative at the United Nations Hosayn Aziz said

---

[4] "The Durand Line, A historic, disputed border separates Afghanistan and Pakistan," *National Geography* https://education.nationalgeographic.org/resource/durand-line/

[5] Asad Munir, "The Faqir of Ipi of North Waziristan," *The Express Tribune*, 2010 https://tribune.com.pk/story/77388/the-faqir-of-ipi-of-north-waziristan

on November 28, 1947, "we cannot recognize the North-West Frontier as part of Pakistan so long as the people of the North-West Frontier have not been given an opportunity free from any kind of influence and I repeat, free from any kind of influence, to determine for themselves whether they wish to be independent or to become a part of Pakistan."[6] Although the negative vote was subsequently withdrawn but the seed of mistrust was planted in the initial days of bilateral relations.[7]

Since then, Afghanistan has never formally recognized the Durand Line as the official border and has frequently clashed with Pakistan over this issue. The Durand Line is a 2,640 km long boundary line between Pakistan and Afghanistan. The agreement was signed in Kabul between the Afghan ruler Amir Abdur Rahman Khan and the British Indian Foreign Secretary Sir Mortimer Durand on November 12th, 1893.

After Pakistan's independence, Kabul demanded the reformation of the Durand line to avoid a divide of Pushtun tribes. Afghan authorities believe that the Durand Line agreement was concluded for 100 years and the validity of the Durand line expired in 1993 and it was demarcated by force by the Britishers. Furthermore, the Afghan authorities also claimed that all the agreements concluded with the British government have become dead and illegal after the emergence of Pakistan because the agreement was originally concluded with British Indian authorities, not with

---

[6] Amin Tarzi and Robert D. Lamb, "Measuring Perceptions About the Pashtun People," *Center for Strategic and International Studies*, 2011
https://csis-website-prod.s3.amazonaws.com/s3fs-public/legacy_files/files/publication/110316_Lamb_PashtunPerceptions_web.pdf

[7] Dr Muhammad Ali and Malik Safdar, "Pakistan Afghan Relation History Conflicts and challenges," *Pak. Journal of Int'L Affairs*, Vol 3, Issue 2 (2020)

Pakistani authorities.[8] Pakistan several times stated that the Durand Line issue is a settled one and that there is nothing more to discuss on it while Kabul declared the Durand Line to be an imaginary line.[9] Pakistan said that the Durand Treaty did not have any time limit. It was not signed for 100 years, or any other time frame.

Pakistan also rejects Afghanistan's point of view on the ground that Afghans cannot invalidate the legal aspect of international laws. Pakistan said that border cannot be restructured or nullified because the Vienna Convention on Succession of States on Respect of Treaties (VCSSRT)[10] has unanimously endorsed 'uti possidetis juris', which says that bilateral treaties with or between colonial powers pass on to the descendant sovereign states. The transfer of power from one country to another like from Britain to Pakistan or Britain to India didn't change the legal status of the Durand line or any agreement. The law 'res transit cum suo onere' decodes[11] that all agreements of the extinct state regarding the borderline stay legitimate.

From 1809 to 1947, Afghan authority and British rulers

---

[8] Brad L Brasseur, "Recognising the Durand Line: A Way Forward for Afghanistan and Pakistan?," *The East West Institute*, 2011

[9] "Splintering relations?: Durand Line is a 'settled issue', says FO," *The Express Tribune*, 2012 https://tribune.com.pk/story/456881/splintering-relations-durand-line-is-a-settled-issue-says-fo/

[10] "Vienna Convention on Succession of States in respect of Treaties," *UN*, 1978 https://legal.un.org/ilc/texts/instruments/english/conventions/3_2_1978.pdf

[11] "Res transit cum suo onere" *Oxford Reference* https://www.oxfordreference.com/display/10.1093/acref/9780195369380.001.0001/acref-9780195369380-e-1847;jsessionid=3EDA2061E43A65A6EBD7C98E15BA2427#:~:text=%E2%80%9CA%20thing%20passes%20away%20with,the%20territory%20or%20property%20itself.

signed numerous agreements and treaties, but the Durand line agreement was the most popular. The agreement allowed Afghanistan to relinquish some of its sovereignty over some frontier districts, while giving it control over other districts over which it had previously little control.

After Amir Abdul Rahman's death, his son Amir Habibullah reaffirmed all of his father's arrangements and agreements with Britain, including accepting the Durand Line.[12] He also reaffirmed with Britain in 1919 at Rawalpindi and in 1921 at Kabul all previously agreed upon border arrangements between Afghanistan and India. In 1930, under King Mohammad Nadir, Afghanistan reaffirmed the 1921 Anglo-Afghan treaty signed at Kabul, thereby recognising the Durand Line as a border between Afghanistan and India.[13]

British governments have also endorsed Pakistan's stance on the issue. The British Secretary of State for the Commonwealth Relations, Philip Noel-Baker, with reference to the then North West Frontier Province (NWFP) territory, said in 1950 that "it is His Majesty's view that Pakistan is in international law the inheritor of the rights and duties of the old government of India and of His Majesty's government in the United Kingdom, in these territories, and that the Durand Line is the international frontier." [14] Pakistan's stance was also supported by other countries as well as the members of the Southeast Asia Treaty Organisation (SEATO). In their ministerial meeting held in Karachi in March 1956, "the council declared that their governments recognised

---

[12] Arka Biswas," Durand Line: History, Legality & Future," *Occasional Paper,* 2013

[13] Arwin Rahi, "The Durand Line: Separating myth from reality," *The Express Tribune*, 2022 https://tribune.com.pk/article/97542/the-durand-line-separating-myth-from-reality

[14] Olaf Caroe, "The Pathans." *Oxford University Press*, 1958

that the sovereignty of Pakistan extends up to the Durand Line, the international boundary between Pakistan and Afghanistan."[15]

Pashtun independence is another significant topic that has strained ties between the two nations. There is a large number of people on both sides of the Durand Line who belongs to an ethnic group known as the Pashtuns. Despite being split up into numerous intricate tribes and subtribes, the Pashtuns have a common language, customs, history and culture. Pashtun nationalists in Afghanistan have campaigned for the establishment of a separate Pashtun state for Pakistani Pashtun or the specific area that should be merged with Afghanistan. It can be said that the demands of the Afghan government were changing frequently as initially they didn't accept the Durand line but they demand a separate Pashtun state. Later on, they demanded that Pashtun ethnic area should be merged with Afghanistan. Afghanistan has always embraced the notion of a unified Pashtunistan as a means of annexing the Pashtun-majority regions of Pakistan. On the other side, Pakistan has strongly rejected the idea of an independent Pashtunistan. The Afghan government has been charged by the Pakistani government for harbouring and aiding Pashtun separatists within its borders.

In 1948, Pashtunistan propaganda was at its peak. In his inaugural speech in Shin-a-i-Milli in 1948, King Zahir Shah made the following remarks about the Pashtunistan issue: "The Afghan nation welcomed and viewed with utmost gratification the establishment of the dominion of Pakistan and India and the Afghan government did not fail in exerting their best efforts to take up the matter of our Afghan brethren living in the government of Great Britain and the newly set up

---

[15] Shireen Mazari, "The Durand Line: Evolution of an International Frontier," *Strategic Studies* vol. 2, no. 2 (Autumn 1978): 45

government of Pakistan. Whilst we have openly declared our desire to set up an embassy of Afghanistan in Karachi, with a view to cementing the relations of friendship and "Bon Voisinage" with Pakistan. We earnestly hope that assurances in this regard will be fully implemented."[16]

Mirza Ali Khan alias the Faqir of Ipi is one of the leading personalities in the Tribal region. He played a key role in the resistance against the Britishers. He belongs to North Waziristan. A large number of freedom fighters from far and wide joined him against British imperialism. British forces suffered heavy losses during their fights with the freedom fighters of the Faqir of Ipi. He was against the British Empire initially but after the independence, he also raised guns against Pakistan. He was of the view that the white Englishmen have left brown Englishmen behind in Pakistan and tribal people should fight them. His objective was to establish an independent state of 'Pakhtunistan'. He was also in touch with Afghanistan and India.

For achieving this objective, he also established a Pashtun assembly with two chapters: the first was in Tirah headed by Afridis and the second was in Waziristan. In 1949, he called a tribal jirga in Gurwek and demanded that the government of Pakistan recognise the independent state of Pashtunistan.[17] He also sent a handout in this regard to the United Nations. Its meetings were held at different locations in Afghanistan, which no doubt had secret Afghan

---

[16] Abdul Manan Bazai, "An Assessment of Pak-Afghan Relations, Since 1947 Up to 2001," *University of Balochistan*, 2008, p 25 http://prr.hec.gov.pk/jspui/bitstream/123456789/877/1/1899S.pdf

[17] Mohammad Hussain Hunarmal, "The formidable Faqir," *The News*, 2021 https://www.thenews.com.pk/tns/detail/789500-the-formidable-faqir

support.[18] Kabul, along with Afghan areas and other parts of the Tribal region, raised a Pakhtunistan flag.[19] The Afghan government declared August 31 to be Pashtunistan Day, which has since been formally celebrated on that date every year.[20]

In 1950, Afghanistan and Pakistan also engaged in armed clashes in the area of Gwazha, north of Quetta. On September 30, 1950, a large Afghan force invaded Pakistan in Deobandi area, about 30 miles northeast of Chaman.[21] With artillery support, the Afghan army occupied a strategic pass aimed at cutting off the Chaman-Quetta rail line. In the end, however, after a bloody week of fighting, the Pakistani army retook the pass.[22]

Due to the uprising, Pakistan sent off its troops and bombed some Pashtun villages. As part of this event, the Afghan government also alleged that Pakistan bombed a village within its borders. Later on, at the start of the 1950s, his rebel movement finally collapsed because he was not getting enough support from the tribal elders as elders believed that the Jihad was against the Britishers which ended when they left.[23]

Several events that occurred in the early stages of the bilateral ties had a direct influence on them. On October 16, 1951, one of the key events happened. Said Akbar

---

[18] Dr Baber Shah, "Geo-Strategic Patterns of a post-Taliban Afghanistan, *Strategic Studies*, Islamabad, 2002, p.45

[19] "Pashtunistan - 1947-1955," *Global Security* https://www.globalsecurity.org/military/world/war/pashtunistan-1947.htm#google_vignette

[20] Ibid

[21] "Pashtunistan - 1947-1955," *Global Security* https://www.globalsecurity.org/military/world/war/pashtunistan-1947.htm

[22] Ibid

[23] Ibid

Babrak, an Afghan national, shot and killed Pakistani Prime Minister Liaquat Ali Khan in Rawalpindi.[24]It should be noted that the accused was Babrak's son, the chief of the Zadran Tribe in Khost, Afghanistan.[25] While defending Amanullah, Said Akbar's father was killed in a battle. Said Akbar was a Brigadier in the Afghan Army.[26] Being pro-Ammanullah faction, the family had become persona-non-grata . In January 1947, Said Akbar fled to India. The Indian government decided to provide him and his family members political refuge, along with a place to live and a monthly stipend. He was then residing in Abbottabad.

The Afghan government immediately refuted Akbar's actions and claimed that he had already lost his Afghan citizenship as a result of his anti-national activities. They also claimed that the British colonial authorities in pre-partition India had given Akbar asylum in the North Western Frontier Province, but that his past and citizenship had a direct impact on the relationship between the two states.[27]

Pakistani officials made a number of recommendations about the reasons behind his actions. Some thought the murderer was a religious fundamentalist, whilst others said Said Akbar was angry of Liaquat Ali Khan's Kashmir Policy because it prevented him from engaging in jihad

---

[24] Syed Muhammad Zulqurnain Zaidi, "The Assassination of the Prime Minister Liaquat Ali Khan: The Fateful Journey," *National Institute of Historical & Cultural Research*, p. 2

[25] Ibid

[26] Syed Muhammad Zulqurnain Zaidi, "The Assassination of the Prime Minister Liaquat Ali Khan: The Fateful Journey," *National Institute of Historical & Cultural Research*, p. 3 http://www.nihcr.edu.pk/Latest_English_Journal/4.%20THE%20ASSASSINATION.pdf

[27] Akhtar Balouch, "The mystery that shrouds Liaquat Ali Khan's murder," *Dawn*, 2015 https://www.dawn.com/news/1213461

against India. Numerous explanations have been advanced over the years, including the participation of foreign intelligence services and the case has never been entirely resolved. The killing of Liaquat Ali Khan's exact circumstances have never been fully established and the investigation is still active.

Another important factor in Pakistani Prime Minister Liaqat's murdering time was the increasing intensity in the emerging Cold war and subsequently starting of war in the Korean Peninsula and security alliances formation in the international arena. Pakistan preferred to join the United States block. While Afghanistan was inclined towards the Union of Soviet Socialist Republics (USSR). Due to Indo-Afghan Nexus, Pakistan's joined Southeast Asia Treaty Organization (SEATO) in 1954 and Central Treaty Organization, or CENTO in 1959 for defence purposes. Afghanistan also raises concerns about the joining of Pakistan's regional security alliance sponsored by the United States.[28]

Prime Minister Sardar Mohammed Daoud Khan (1953–1963) was considered, one of the anti-Pakistan. Mr. Daoud was very vocal against Pakistan on the Durand line and Pashtunistan issue. He also interfered in the internal politics of Pakistan. Consequently, the era of Daoud had a number of unpleasant episodes, including fights over border security, disturbances at embassies, a trade embargo, the burning of national flags and embassies, etc.[29]

The Pakistani government announced the One Unit Scheme in 1955, a scheme that merged the four

---

[28] Abdul Manan Bazai, "An Assessment of Pak-Afghan Relations, Since 1947 Up to 2001," University of Balochistan, 2008, p 1 http://prr.hec.gov.pk/jspui/bitstream/123456789/877/1/1899S.pdf

[29] Abdul Manan Bazai, "An assessment of Pak-Afghan relations, Since 1947 up to 2001," p. 27 http://prr.hec.gov.pk/jspui/bitstream/123456789/877/1/1899S.pdf

western provinces of Balochistan, Khyber Pakhtunkhwa (that time NWFP), Punjab and Sindh into one single administrative unit, West Pakistan. East Pakistan was to be the second administrative unit. The government's main objective was to run both east and west Pakistan smoothly, but it was met with widespread opposition and protest, especially among Pashtuns. Pashtuns in Afghanistan also saw this scheme as an attack on their ethnic identity, escalating tensions between the two countries.

Pakistan's decision to merge the provinces of West Pakistan into a single Pashtun administrative unit was denounced by the Afghan government. The Pakistani Embassy in Kabul was attacked by angry Afghan mobs following riots in Afghanistan. Pakistan's diplomatic missions in Kabul, Qandahar and Jalalabad were attacked in March 1955 and the Pashtunistan flag was hoisted on the Pakistan Embassy's chancery. In reaction, protests and counter-protests were also held in Karachi, Peshawar and other cities of Pakistan. The Afghan transit trade facility was also suspended, the border remained closed and fighting erupted. Pakistan closed Afghan consulates and trade agencies in Peshawar, Quetta and Chaman in May 1955, banning Afghan employees from the areas. The tensions eventually subsided and the two countries resumed their normal trade and diplomatic relations. The resumption was facilitated through mediation by Egypt, Saudi Arabia, Iran and Turkey.[30]

The One Unit Scheme was eventually abolished in 1970, after the 1970 Pakistan general elections in which the Awami League, which had campaigned for the abolition of the one unit, won a majority in the West

---

[30] Dr Muhammad Ali and Malik Safdar, "Pakistan Afghan Relation History Conflicts and challenges," *Pak. Journal of Int'L Affairs,* Vol 3, Issue 2 (2020), p. 405

Pakistan assembly. The abolishment of the One Unit Scheme led to the formation of the separate provinces of Punjab, Balochistan, Khyber Pakhtunkhwa and Sindh.

Later, when Hussain Shaheed Suharwardy, Pakistan's prime minister, and Iskandar Mirza, Pakistan's president, visited Afghanistan in August 1956, the relationship improved and diplomatic contacts were strengthened. In February 1958, King Zahir Shah,[31] and Prime Minister Sardar Daoud Khan in 1959 travelled to Pakistan. These encounters aided in establishing a spirit of amity on both sides. However, these cordial ties did not last for very long.

Pakistani and Afghan forces were once more engaged in combat in the Bajaur region in 1961. Because of the too much violence, Pakistan's government finally issued an order for Afghanistan to shut down its consulates and commercial offices there while also announcing the closure of its consulates in Kandahar and Jalalabad. Pakistan warned the Afghan government that normal diplomatic contacts couldn't continue because of unusual conditions on the border.

The diplomatic skirmish was at its height and each side was pointing the finger at the other. But the Afghan government insists that Pakistan change its stance. Afghanistan, a landlocked nation, also feels uneasy since Pakistan was the shortest and least expensive path for it to trade and port.[32] In response to the Shah of

---

[31] "In February 1958, Mohammad Zahir Shah, the king of Afghanistan, visited India after an official visit to Pakistan," *Global Indian.* https://www.globalindian.com/galleryandvideos/global-indian-museum/mohammad-zahir-shah-visited-india-1958/

[32] Abdul Manan Bazai, "An assessment of Pak-Afghan relations, Since 1947 up to 2001," p. 27 http://prr.hec.gov.pk/jspui/bitstream/123456789/877/1/1899S.pdf

Iran's mediation, the trade embargoes were quickly abolished. It must be acknowledged that the Afghan prime minister, Sardar Mohammed Daoud Khan, was a major factor in escalating the conflict, but things improved once King Zahir Shah removed him from office on 17 July 1973.[33]

As a consequence of Iran's effective mediation, which led to the 1963 Tehran Accord, Afghanistan and Pakistan decided to re-establish diplomatic connections, reopen their closed borders and begin trade and economic relationships to foster an atmosphere of goodwill, friendliness and mutual confidence. Both nations also agreed to settle all of their disagreements peacefully and in accordance with international law while promoting goodwill and trust between one another. When Pakistan and India went to war in 1965, the ties between the two countries had improved to the point where Afghanistan supported Pakistan, allowing Pakistan to focus entirely on its conflict with India and to worry less about the security of its western border.

King Zahir Shah visited Pakistan in the spring of 1967, after President Ayub Khan's January 1966 trip to Kabul.[34] The disagreements over the Durand line and Pashtunistan, however, were not resolved. Kabul also welcomed Islamabad's move to dissolve one unit, which improved Pak-Afghan ties even more. Afghanistan also exercised restraint and stayed completely neutral during

---

[33] "Mohammad Zahir Shah (1933–73)," *Britannica* https://www.britannica.com/place/Afghanistan/Mohammad-Zahir-Shah-1933-73

[34] Arwin Rahi, "Afghanistan and Pakistan's oft-ignored history – 1947-1978," *The Express Tribune*, September, 10, 2020 https://tribune.com.pk/article/97165/afghanistan-and-pakistans-oft-ignored-history-1947-1978

the 1971 Indo-Pakistan War.[35]

While the relations were going smoothly then suddenly there was some internal political crisis happened in Afghanistan. As a result of a bloodless military coup, Sardar Daoud Khan overthrew King Zahir Shah and declared himself president on July 17, 1973. During that time, King Zahir was visiting Europe. As soon as Daud Khan took power, he suppressed the left and lessened the country's dependence on the Soviet Union, which the Soviets didn't like. The Durand Line and Pashtunistan were again brought up. Daoud Khan established an iron fist dictatorship in Afghanistan for the next four years. The two countries had relatively cordial relations before the coup, with both countries cooperating on issues such as trade and water management. Pashtuns saw Daoud's government as representing their interests, which resulted in tensions between Pashtuns and Pakistanis. [36] The tension increased after revelation of Kabul's providing arms and ammunition to Pashtun and Baloch separatists. A guerrilla camp was formed near Pak Afghan border.[37] Kabul offered refuge to those who managed to flee an army operation in Baluchistan. [38] Famous rebel commanders that made it to Afghanistan were Asfandyar Wali Khan, Sardar Attaullah Mengal, Sardar

---

[35] Rafiullah Kakar, "Pak-Afghan Relations: Tracing the Roots of Troubled Past (1947-2001)," *Journal of Asian Politics & History*, 2012

[36] Hussain Haqqani, "Pakistan: Between the Mosque and the Military," op. cit,170.

[37] Tehseena Usman, "Trust Deficit in Pak-Afghan Relations and its Implications: A Historical Perspective (1947-2001)," p 9 https://www.qurtuba.edu.pk/thedialogue/The%20Dialogue/8_3/Dialogue_July_September2013_303-326.pdf

[38] Hussain Haqqani, "Pakistan: Between the Mosque and the Military," Carnegie Endowment for International Peace, 2005. op. cit, 170.

Khair Bakhsh Marri, and Ajmal Khattak. Pushtunistan Day was also observed by the administration of Daud on August 30, 1973.[39] Pakistan's security was severely threatened by Afghanistan's unrelenting backing for the Pushtun and Baluch insurgencies. As a result, the new Kabul government was denounced as anti-Islamic and anti-Pakistan by Pakistan's Prime Minister Zulfiqar Ali Bhutto.

In February 1974, Afghan President Daoud did not attend the 'OIC Leaders' Summit' in Lahore.[40]Daoud not only exacted vengeance on his adversary, but also imprisoned, murdered, and banished a number of traditionalists and Islamists. During Daud's leadership, more than 600 Islamists were murdered.[41] Traditionalist and former prime minister Mohammad Hashim Maiwandwal died in the police custody.[42]

Professor Ghulam Mohammad Niyazi, a renowned Islamist, was imprisoned and eventually slain. While numerous other Islamist leaders escaped to Peshawar.[43] Among them were Tajik Professor Burhanuddin Rabbani (Jamat e Islami), his follower

---

[39] Anthony Arnold, "Afghanistan Two Party Communism: Parcham and Khalaq," California: Hoover Institution Press, 1985, p 45.

[40] Hanif-ur-Rahman, "Pak-Afghan Relations during Z.A. Bhutto Era: The Dynamics of Cold War," *Pakistan Journal of History and Culture*, Vol. XXXIII, No.2, 2012, p 10 http://www.nihcr.edu.pk/Latest_English_Journal/Jrnl%2033-2%20(2012)%20PDF/2.%20Pak-Afghan%20Relations,%20hanif%20khan.pdf

[41] Tehseena Usman, "Trust Deficit in Pak-Afghan Relations and its Implications: A Historical Perspective (1947-2001)," p 10 https://www.qurtuba.edu.pk/thedialogue/The%20Dialogue/8_3/Dialogue_July_September2013_303-326.pdf

[42] Ibid

[43] Oliver Roy, "Islam and Resistance in Afghanistan," Cambridge University Press,

Ahmad Shah Masoud and Gulbadin Hikmatyar, founder of Hezb-i-Islami (Party of Islam).[44] Islamists sought to restructure Afghan society and create a contemporary political philosophy based on Islam.

Prime Minister Bhutto authorised a tit-for-tat action against Afghanistan. Naseerullah Babar, the Inspector General for the Frontier Corps (IGFC) was given the duty of preparing Afghan dissidents to act as proxies within Afghanistan.[45] After a 26-year-long proxy war waged by Afghanistan in the name of Pashtunistan, it was seen as Pakistan's first deployment of proxies against Afghanistan.

Meanwhile, Bhutto backed Islamists on geopolitical rather than ideological grounds. Gulbadin Hikmatyar and Ahmad Shah Masoud, two young Afghan student leaders, may launch an attack on Daud's authority.[46] Pakistan also taught 5000 Afghan dissidents in combat, wireless communication and guerrilla tactics in covert military camps. There were 1,331 Afghan citizens and their families on a list sent to the Pakistani embassy in Kabul in 1974 for monthly stipends.[47] In 1974, rebels plotted a coup with the support of Pakistan but Daud discovered their plot and imprisoned those involved.[48]

In reaction to bomb attacks in Pakistan, Afghan Islamists

---

[44] Angelo Rasanayagam, "Afghanistan: A Modern History," I.B. Tauris, p. 103

[45] Sultan M Hali, "Breaking the myths of Pakistan ruining Afghanistan," *Pakistan Today* https://archive.pakistantoday.com.pk/2016/08/12/breaking-the-myths-of-pakistan-ruining-afghanistan/

[46] Tehseena Usman, "Trust Deficit in Pak-Afghan Relations and its Implications: A Historical Perspective (1947-2001)," p 11 https://www.qurtuba.edu.pk/thedialogue/The%20Dialogue/8_3/Dialogue_July_September2013_303-326.pdf

[47] Imtiaz Gul, "The Unholy Nexus: Pak-Afghan relations Under the Taliban," Vanguard, 2002, 11-12

[48] Ibid

staged an insurrection in Panjshir Valley (northeast of Kabul) in July 1975, attacking two police stations and holding much of the valley for three days before fleeing to Pakistan. Daud blamed Pakistan for orchestrating the insurrection.[49]

The National Awami Party (NAP) was active from the 1950s to the 1970s, in Pakistan. It had leftist and nationalist ideologies and was influential in Balochistan and Khyber Pakhtunkhwa. The Afghan government was very close to it. During the Cold War era when both countries were receiving support from rival superpowers, the Afghan government provided some financial assistance to NAP.[50] The ex-Governor of the NWFP, Hayat Khan Sherpao, was killed in a bomb blast in February 1975.[51] According to reports, the NAP militant wing allegedly carried out the assassination. Awami Party (NAP) was barred twice from active politics by the incumbent rulers for participating in anti-state activities.[52] Despite being banned, they continued their political activities and formed a new party called Awami National Party (ANP).[53]

---

[49] Ibid

[50] Hanif-ur-Rahman, "Pak-Afghan Relations during Z.A. Bhutto Era: The Dynamics of Cold War," *Pakistan Journal of History and Culture*, Vol. XXXIII, No.2, 2012, p 9 http://www.nihcr.edu.pk/Latest_English_Journal/Jrnl%2033-2%20(2012)%20PDF/2.%20Pak-Afghan%20Relations,%20hanif%20khan.pdf

[51] Sultan M Hali, "Breaking the myths of Pakistan ruining Afghanistan," *Pakistan Today* https://archive.pakistantoday.com.pk/2016/08/12/breaking-the-myths-of-pakistan-ruining-afghanistan/

[52] Sabir Shah, "NAP was banned twice by Yahya and Bhutto," *The News*, 2015 https://www.thenews.com.pk/print/38435-nap-was-banned-twice-by-yahya-and-bhutto

[53] Ibid

Both nations resolved to pursue reconciliation when the internal security situation in both countries worsened to an alarming degree in 1976. They exchanged high-level visits and resolved to resolve their concerns, particularly the lengthy Trust Deficit in Islamabad-Kabul relations and its Implications.

Sardar Daoud visited Pakistan for four days from August 20 to 24, 1976, at the invitation of Zulfikar Ali Bhutto.[54] He also visited Pakistan the next year. During his visit, he asked Pakistani authorities to free inmates of Pashtun ethnicity or who had raised weapons against Pakistan.[55] There was some counter-visitation from the Pakistani side as well, but it remained official and brought no fresh developments. Later, both nations' relations deteriorate as a result of the internal political conflict. In a military revolution led by Zia ul Haq in 1977, Bhutto was overthrown, and communist troops overthrew Daud in April 1978. During the Soviet-sponsored "Saur Revolution," Afghan president Daud and his whole family were slaughtered.[56] Kabul was taken over by the People's Democratic Party of Afghanistan (PDPA), Noor Mohammed Taraki was appointed as its president, Hafiz Ullah Amin as its prime minister and Babrak Karmal as its deputy prime minister. Afghanistan's name was changed to the Democratic

---

[54] Arwin Rahi, "Afghanistan and Pakistan's oft-ignored history – 1947-1978," *The Express Tribune*, September, 10, 2020 https://tribune.com.pk/article/97165/afghanistan-and-pakistans-oft-ignored-history-1947-1978

[55] Tehseena Usman, "Trust Deficit in Pak-Afghan Relations and its Implications: A Historical Perspective (1947-2001)"

[56] Sultan M Hali, "Breaking the myths of Pakistan ruining Afghanistan, " *Pakistan Today* https://archive.pakistantoday.com.pk/2016/08/12/breaking-the-myths-of-pakistan-ruining-afghanistan/

Republic of Afghanistan (DRA).[57]

Afghanistan saw the Saur Revolution started in on April 27, 1978, a communist uprising that was headed by the People's Democratic Party of Afghanistan (PDPA). The name of the revolution comes from the month it occurred according to the Afghan calendar (Saur being the name of the month).[58] In a coup d'état, the PDPA, led by Nur Muhammad Taraki, seized control and installed a communist regime. Resistance to the revolution came from a number of parties, including traditionalists, Islamists and other leftist organisations, which finally sparked a protracted and bloody civil war. Later on, there were some internal differences within the political party. Khalq was more radical than Parcham under Noor Mohammad Taraki and Amin. Political, social and economic transformations were what they sought to achieve. [59]

Babrak Karmal led the Parchamities, which supported gradual reform in the face of growing difficulties. A significant turning point in Afghan history, the Saur Revolution had a significant influence on the nation's politics, society, and economy. The new pro-Communist government declared that Pashtunistan will receive full backing. Pakistan, which had always backed the Afghan monarchy, considered the uprising a serious security concern.

In addition, as a result of the revolution, a large number of Afghan refugees entered Pakistan, straining its resources and escalating tensions between the two

---

[57] Abdul Manan Bazai, "An assessment of Pak-Afghan relations, Since 1947 up to 2001," p.69
http://prr.hec.gov.pk/jspui/bitstream/123456789/877/1/1899S.pdf
[58] Ibid
[59] Abdul Manan Bazai, "An assessment of Pak-Afghan relations, Since 1947 up to 2001," p. 79
http://prr.hec.gov.pk/jspui/bitstream/123456789/877/1/1899S.pdf

nations. The situation in Afghanistan in general and the significant refugee population on Pakistani land in particular have given rise to a number of complex issues including the economy, politics, society, strategy and weaponry. A significant factor in Pakistan's rising crime rate is the easy access to enormous numbers of illegally obtained and smuggled guns and ammunition.

The revolution also sent a wave of Afghan migrants into Pakistan, straining its resources and escalating tensions between the two nations. The overall Afghan crisis and the high number of refugees who have landed in Pakistan in particular have given rise to a number of intricate issues including the economy, politics, society, strategy, and weaponry. A significant factor in Pakistan's rising crime rate is the easy access to enormous numbers of illegally obtained and smuggled guns and ammunition.

Tensions between Afghanistan and Pakistan were further made worse by the Soviet Union's decision to intervene in Afghanistan in 1979.[60] When the USSR invaded Afghanistan, Pakistan's approach to the Afghanistan changed significantly. The region's character was significantly altered after the Soviet invasion. The whole Persian Gulf area was directly threatened by the Red Army in addition to Pakistan. Perhaps there was concern that the Soviets would have utilised Afghanistan as a gateway to the Indian Ocean.

The Soviet Union invaded Afghanistan in December 1979 with the specific intention of assisting the communist administration that the Saur Revolution had brought to power. Pakistan, who saw the presence of Soviet forces in Afghanistan as a direct danger to its own security, considered this invasion as being a serious

---

[60] "Soviet invasion of Afghanistan," *Britannica* https://www.britannica.com/event/Soviet-invasion-of-Afghanistan

threat.

Pakistan's response to the Soviet invasion was to help the mujahideen, or Afghan resistance, who were opposing the Soviet-backed regime. The mujahideen received aid from Pakistan in the form of weapons, instruction and safe haven. The mujahideen received weapons and assistance from the US and other Western nations through Pakistan. Pakistan let the CIA and other Western intelligence services transfer weapons and supplies to the mujahideen via its borders.

Pakistan also supported the mujahideen diplomatically by urging other nations to help and support the Afghan struggle. The internal politics of Pakistan was also significantly impacted by the Soviet-Afghan War. The conflict caused a flood of Afghan refugees into Pakistan, straining its resources and causing economic instability. As more young men joined the mujahideen to fight in Afghanistan, the battle also increased religious extremism and militancy in Pakistan.

Previously, the Afghan forces were too ineffective to create a significant danger to Pakistan, allowing Z.A. Bhutto and subsequently President Zia to continue their Afghan Policy independently and without the help of any foreign power. But after the Soviet military in Afghanistan situation goes worst. According to Mr Abdul Sattar, ex-Foreign Minister of Pakistan,

"The Soviet military intervention provoked a deep sense of alarm in Pakistan. Suddenly the buffer disappeared and if the Soviet rulers consolidated their control in Afghanistan, they could use it as a springboard to reach the warm waters of the Arabian Sea. Pakistan could not afford to acquiesce in the Soviet intervention. But neither could it afford a confrontation with a superpower. Islamabad, therefore, decided on the middle course, avoiding confrontation but raising a low-pitched voice of concern and protest."[61]

To combat the threat posed by the USSR, Pakistan, the US, China, and Arab nations banded together. They did this by supporting the legitimate Afghan resistance movement that was already active in Afghanistan. The Afghan resistance movement, which was composed of numerous factions, fought the Soviet soldiers and their Afghan allies with the help of finances from the USA and Arab governments, technical assistance from the CIA,[62] weaponry from China, and training and coordination support from Pakistan intelligence agency ISI.[63] From $60 million yearly in 1981 to $400 million in 1984, the covert aid for acquiring, educating, supplying, and overseeing Mujahideen on the battlefield.[64] President Carter, on May 4, 1980, stated, "We will provide military equipment, food and other assistance to help Pakistan defend its independence and national security against the seriously increased threat from the north."[65]

There were seven Major Mujahideen groups based in Afghanistan who were supported by Pakistan. They were:

1. Hizb-e-Islami of Gulbadin Kikmatyar,
2. Hizb-e-Islami Khalis of Mohammad Yunus Khalis

---

[61] Abdul Sattar, "Afghanistan: Past, Present and Future, From Jihad to Civil War", *The Institute of Regional Studies, Islamabad,* 1997, pp. 462-63

[62] Sultan M Hali, "Breaking the myths of Pakistan ruining Afghanistan," *Pakistan Today* https://archive.pakistantoday.com.pk/2016/08/12/breaking-the-myths-of-pakistan-ruining-afghanistan/

[63] Dennis Kux, "The United States and Pakistan, 1947-2000: Disenchanted Allies," Woodrow Wilson, 2001, p. 252

[64] Dennis Kux, "The United States and Pakistan, 1947-2000: Disenchanted Allies," Woodrow Wilson, 2001, op. cit, p. 274

[65] Dennis Kux, "The United States and Pakistan, 1947-2000: Disenchanted Allies," Woodrow Wilson, 2001, op. cit, p. 247

3. Jamiat-e-Islami of Burhanuddin Rabbani
4. Ittehad-e-Islami of Ustad Abdul Rasul Sayyaf
5. Harakat-e-Inqilabi of Maulvi Mohammed Nabi Mohammedi
6. Mahaz-e-Milli by Pir Syed Ahmed Gailani and
7. Jabha-e-Milli by Sibghatullah Mojeddidi.

The Hizb-e-Islami and Ittehade-Islami were fundamentalists. The remaining three, Harakat-e Inqilabi, Mahaze-e-Milli and Jabha-e-Milli were moderates. There were also some Iran-back proxies.[66] The proxy and guerrilla war were played everywhere in Afghanistan which Mujahaddin were leading. There were also some back talks but that was not working. The world was looking towards Afghanistan. Pakistan as the centre of the game was leading and Mujahaddin was burned with religious sentiments. However, USSR didn't survive and went towards the end of the era.

The Soviet Union withdrew its forces from Afghanistan after a decade of warfare in 1989. The cost of the war in terms of human lives and material resources had grown, and there was also growing domestic resistance inside the Soviet Union to the war. The conflict, which had come to represent Soviet imperialism, had also hurt the Soviet Union's reputation abroad. The Geneva Accords, which were signed between the Soviet Union and Afghanistan in 1988, called for the departure of Soviet forces from Afghanistan. The final Soviet soldiers left Afghanistan on February 15, 1989. The Soviet-Afghan War came to an end with the Soviet Union's army withdrawal, which also played a role in the Soviet Union's final demise in 1991.

---

[66] Abdul Manan Bazai, "An assessment of Pak-Afghan relations, Since 1947 up to 2001," p. 109
http://prr.hec.gov.pk/jspui/bitstream/123456789/877/1/1899S.pdf

CHAPTER 2

TALIBAN AS A POLITICAL PHENOMENON IN AFGHAN POLITICS

Following the withdrawal of the formal Soviet Union from Afghanistan in 1989, new chaos emerged. Although the Soviet withdrawal ended a decade-long occupation in Afghanistan, it also created a power vacuum in the country and created a new civil war between the militant factions. By leaving behind the necessary war equipment and munitions, the Soviets enhanced the staying power of Dr Najeeb Ullah's Government in Kabul until 1992. Meanwhile, westerners and Arabs stopped providing weapons, ammunition and equipment to the Mujaheddin.

Although the Najeeb government remain in power for a few years, during this era the war lords were fighting towards each other and also standing at the doors of Kabul. Here it is to be mentioned, that there was no concept of Taliban at that time and the Afghan society was lawless and there were no rules and laws and the area was divided between different warlords. Najeebullah resigned[67] from his post on April 16, 1992 and later on, sought asylum at the UN compound in

[67] "Najeebullah announces to tender resignation," *Afghan Islamic Press*, 19 March, 1992 https://www.afghanislamicpress.com/en/news/32063

Kabul, but was later arrested by the Taliban and executed on 27 September 1996.

It was expected that there would be a lot of bloodshed since three major Mujhideen commanders had their eyes on Kabul: Ahmad Shah Massoud, Gulbuddin Hekmatyar and Abdul Rashid Dostum. By initiating talks between them, Pakistan played a key role in moving Afghanistan out of its power vacuum.

In 1992, Mujahideen leaders and Pakistani government officials-initiated talks in Peshawar. Based on the April 1992 Peshawar Accord,[68] an interim government was formed. The accord was signed by all party leaders except Gulbuddin Hekmatyar. Due to friction between Pushtun and non-Pushtun parties, Pakistani officials maintained a neutral stance.

In the Peshawar Accord, Sibghatullah Mojaddedi was appointed acting President for two months, followed by Burhanuddin Rabbani for four months. A Shoora would be held after six months to choose the government for the next eighteen months, followed by elections. A war between Hekmatyar and Massoud for control of Kabul was also ongoing during the talks.[69]

Among the other Afghan competitors in the fight for Kabul, Rabbani and Massoud's forces were the first to seize control of the nation's capital.[70]This has significant ramifications for the stability of the peace in Afghanistan. However, the deal was working since Mojaddedi peacefully handed over power to Burhanuddin Rabbani after two months and Rabbani's interim administration

---

[68] "Peshawar Accord," Peace agreement database

[69] Stephen Tanne, "Afghanistan: A Military History from Alexander the Great to the War against the Taliban," *Da Capo Press,* 2009, p. 276

[70] Ahmed Rashid, "Taliban: Militant Islam, Oil and Fundamentalism in Central Asia Paperback," *Yale University Press,* 2010

was to govern for four months. In order to maintain military control over Kabul while the fighting was ongoing, the new administration was dependent on Massoud and Dostum's army.[71]

While Hekmatyar launched rocket attacks on the city and blasted the administration as a covert communist state, the crisis was further started by Rabbani's refusal to resign as president after four months in office as promised by the Peshawar accord. Instead, in December 1992, he was elected by a false Shoora that was dominated by his loyalists.[72]

The position of prime minister was offered to Hekmatyar, but he declined, arguing that Rabbani's administration lacked legitimacy and that it should not share power with him.[73] Nawaz Sharif, then prime minister of Pakistan, is among the official that also travels to Kabul to hold the talks.[74]

Pakistan then launched fresh efforts to mediate. The so-called Islamabad Accord, which was reached on March 1, 1993, in Islamabad by eight prominent party leaders,[75] permitted Rabbani to finish his 18-month tenure as president while Hekmatyar served as prime minister and Massoud as the defence minister. This agreement was made despite the fact that fierce fighting

---

[71] Abdul Manan Bazai, "An assessment of Pak-Afghan relations, Since 1947 up to 2001," p.148 http://prr.hec.gov.pk/jspui/bitstream/123456789/877/1/1899S.pdf

[72] Larry P. Larry Goodson, "Afghanistan's Endless War: State Failure, Regional Politics, and the Rise of the Taliban," *University of Washington Press*, 2001

[73] Ibid

[74] Abdul Manan Bazai, "An assessment of Pak-Afghan relations, Since 1947 up to 2001," p.149 http://prr.hec.gov.pk/jspui/bitstream/123456789/877/1/1899S.pdf

[75] "Afghan Peace Accord (Islamabad Accord)," Peace agreement database

was also taking place in Kabul. It was a cooperative peace endeavour because the governments of Saudi Arabia and Iran, as well as various Afghan organisations, were also invited. All the leaders departed for Mecca to perform Umrah at the time of the Islamabad accord's signing. However, the warlords did not completely implement this agreement and tensions flared once more.

Hekmatyar's proposed cabinet failed to get support. It was not agreed upon when he demanded that Massoud be removed from his position as defence minister. Again, a civil war broke out throughout the nation. Fighting broke out often between factions that had formed alliances with one another in different, constantly shifting stances, mostly along racial lines. For example, Pushtuns in the South, Uzbeks and Tajiks in the North and Shi'a Hazaras in the centre battled each other.[76]

After Rabbani was elected president again in June 1994, Pakistan this time charged the Afghan leader with abusing his position of authority. When anti-Pakistani demonstrators launched rocket attacks on the Pakistani embassy, ties between Afghanistan and Pakistan also worsened. Rabbani began establishing ties with India, which prompted Islamabad to react angrily.[77]

Kabul was under the jurisdiction of Rabbani, Heart was under Ismael Khan, Mazar-e-Sharif was under Dostum and the south-eastern areas were under Hikmatyar's rule.[78] Nearly all of the Afghan leaders' real faces have been seen by their people. However, people were now

---

[76] Ibid

[77] Rifaat Hussain, "PAKISTAN'S RELATIONS WITH AFGHANISTAN: CONTINUITY AND CHANGE," Institute of Strategic Studies Islamabad, 2002

[78] Abdul Manan Bazai, "An assessment of Pak-Afghan relations, Since 1947 up to 2001," p.168 http://prr.hec.gov.pk/jspui/bitstream/123456789/877/1/1899S.pdf

able to see how quickly their leaders formed and broke partnerships. These Afghan leaders lacked the ability or disposition to turn things around. None of them was able to keep their word, not even keeping the vow made in the Holy Kaaba. Afghanistan was on the verge of collapse since the government's authority did not even reach the nation's capital. The world community seems to have lost interest at this time.

2.1 EMERGENCE OF TALIBAN

There is a famous saying that short-term gain for long-term pain is foolhardy and in the case of Islamabad and Kabul this saying is perfectly implemented. After 1979, Pakistan started playing in the internal affair of Afghanistan. The US, Pakistan as well as Saudi Arabia while countering the USSR in Afghanistan created the mujahedeen and funded them. The alliances didn't think that after they move away from Afghanistan how this militia would be diverted to a productive thing. This led towards the civil war and the new emergence of various militant groups.

In 1994, the Taliban phenomenon began. Mullah Muhammad Omar, the Taliban leader, was born in 1959 in Nauda, Kandahar. His family includes four wives and four children, including two sons and two daughters. In August 1999, one of his daughters was killed. During the early stages of Afghan Jihad, Mullah Omar visited Pakistan for two weeks. He was just an ordinary mujahedeen foot soldier. According to some reports, he was severely injured in one of the battles and he removed one of his eyes with a knife by himself. However, other reports claimed that he was operated on in a hospital near Peshawar.[79] Following the end of the Afghan Jihad and the Soviet withdrawal in 1989, Omar

[79] "Taliban and Mullah Omar," *Daily Lead Pakistan*, July 12, 2020 https://leadpakistan.com.pk/news/taliban-and-mullah-omar/

became the imam of a mosque in a small village in Maiwand, Kandahar. At that time, there was no rule or law and the areas were divided into different warlords. The warlords were the only person who makes rules and break them. Everywhere crime ratio was increasing.[80] The public was already desperate.

In an event, two to three ladies and two young boys were sexually assaulted by warlords in Afghanistan.[81] Mullah Omar was asked to take action by the Afghan people as well. Such incidents exhausted the patience of Mullah Omar and his colleagues. They finally made the decision to act. The areas where the rapes took place were taken over by a total of 55 Taliban led by Mullah Omar.[82] When the Taliban raided the camp, they released the girls and killed the commander. Later on, another squad of Taliban freed young boys over whom two warlords were fighting for the right to sodomize.[83]

The Taliban began cleansing roadblocks, disarming violators and assassinating Afghan bandits. Taliban were portrayed as warlord-busting defenders of the helpless. The Taliban started cleaning up numerous districts after receiving enormous popular backing. Their popularity grew quickly. People start joining them from all around Afghanistan.

Another instance occurred when some Mujahidin leaders in the Kandahar region kidnapped 30 Pakistani trucks carrying enticing cargoes of food, medicine and gifts for the Pakistan-delivered Central Asian States of Tajikistan and Uzbekistan. The Taliban retook the

---

[80] Ibid

[81] Ibid

[82] Abdul Manan Bazai, "An assessment of Pak-Afghan relations, Since 1947 up to 2001," p.170 http://prr.hec.gov.pk/jspui/bitstream/123456789/877/1/1899S.pdf

[83] Ahmed Rashid, "Taliban: Islam, Oil, and the New Great Game in Central Asia, Tauris, 2002, p.18

convoy in about two weeks, executed the leaders and paved the way to central Asia.[84]

Taliban followed a fundamentalist form of Islam derived from the Deobandi tradition. The Taliban also enjoyed support from Pakistani religious elements. The Taliban mainly consisted of Afghan students, who had been educated in Pakistan's religious schools. Their objective was to assist the Afghan Mujahideen in evicting Soviet forces from Afghanistan. After the Jihad against the Soviets ended, they move back to their respective places and start spending their normal life. But after the situation goes worst again and formation of Taliban, this people again start joining the group. The group also gained support from Pashtuns, the largest ethnic group in Afghanistan, who were also tired of the fighting and wanted a return to stability. In October 1994, Mullah Omar was appointed Amir- Leader of the Taliban.[85]

The Taliban's first major military action occurred in October 1994 when it gained control of the Pakistani border town of Spin Boldak and the Pasha weapons stockpile. [86] At the time, Hekmatyar's organisation controlled Spin Boldak. They received a sizable amount of military equipment from the captured weapons, including rockets, ammo, artillery and small guns. After that, Kandahar was taken over by the Taliban without

---

[84] Abdul Manan Bazai, "An assessment of Pak-Afghan relations, Since 1947 up to 2001," p.169
http://prr.hec.gov.pk/jspui/bitstream/123456789/877/1/1899S.pdf

[85] "FACTBOX: Five Facts on Taliban Leader Mullah Mohammad Omar," *Reuters*, November 17, 2008
https://www.reuters.com/article/us-afghan-taliban-omar-idUSTRE4AG1EM20081117

[86] "United Nations Arms Embargoes, Their Impact on Arms Flows and Target Behaviour," *Stockholm International Peace Research Institute,* 2007, p 06
https://www.sipri.org/sites/default/files/files/misc/UNAE/SIPRI07UNAETal.pdf

any resistance. By December 1994, the Taliban had established themselves in Kabul's eastern and northern districts, moving toward the strategic town.[87]

The Taliban took over twelve provinces within three months, opening the road to traffic. Local warlords either fled or surrendered to the Taliban as they marched north towards Kabul. The army of Mullah Omar was moving across Afghanistan. The Taliban saw military success during this period, taking control of numerous significant towns, including Heart in 1995, which resulted in the exile of Ismail Khan in Iran, Jalalabad and Kabul in 1996 and Kunduz in 1997. They also took Mazar-I-Sharif in May 1997, lost it and then retook it in August 1998. They also took Bamiyan in September 1998. The Taliban controlled about 90% of Afghanistan in 1998.[88] The Tajiks were the only group resisting the Taliban, although only in the north.[89]

In 1996, the Taliban, led by Mullah Omar, captured the Afghan capital of Kabul and established the Islamic Emirate of Afghanistan. In a similar year, a shura (council) recognized Mullah Omar as amir-ul-momineen ("commander of the faithful"). Burhanuddin Rabbani, the president in office and his ally Ahmed Shah's soldiers departed Kabul after fall of Kabul. Najibullah, a former communist president, and his brother were publicly hanged by the Taliban as their first action after accusing them of being harsh and anti-Islamic.[90] The bodies of

---

[87] Abdul Manan Bazai, "An Assessment of Pak-Afghan Relations, Since 1947 Up to 2001," *University of Balochistan,* 2008, p 24 http://prr.hec.gov.pk/jspui/bitstream/123456789/877/1/1899S.pdf
[88] "Who are the Taliban?," *BBC*, 12 August 2022 https://www.bbc.com/news/world-south-asia-11451718
[89] "Afghanistan: Crisis of Impunity," Human Rights Watch, July 2001, Vol. 13, No. 3, p.15.
[90] "Ex-president hanged by Taliban after fall of Kabul," *Irish Time*, Sep 28 1996

Najibullah and his brother remained hanged for a total of 24 hours.

2.2 TALIBAN RULE FROM 1996 TO 2001

Taliban arrived intending to rid Afghanistan of criminals. The bureaucratic structure was designed using the terminology of the shura, signifying the Islamic component of government and system of consultation. There were three Shura bodies: a Central Shura in Kandahar, a Kabul Shura, and a Military Shura. All decisions are mainly made by the Supreme Shura in Kandahar.[91] The provincial governors were also chosen.

Taliban published a large number of decrees that were based on their self-described interpretation of Sharia. These laws placed a special emphasis on how women should be treated in society and there were a lot of restrictions on women. All forms of social and recreational activity, work, and education were completely prohibited for women. For male, shaving and wearing western clothes were considered offensive.[92]

While, there is a question here as to why Pakistan supports the Afghan Taliban and how the Taliban came into existence? About the emergence of the Taliban, there are at least two popular views. Initially, the Taliban were viewed as an indigenous movement. This was in response to the brutality and corruption exhibited by Mujahideen commanders.

The opposing viewpoint asserts that Pakistan was

---

https://www.irishtimes.com/news/ex-president-hanged-by-taliban-after-fall-of-kabul-1.90501

[91] Abdul Manan Bazai, "An Assessment of Pak-Afghan Relations, Since 1947 Up to 2001," *University of Balochistan*, 2008, p 175 http://prr.hec.gov.pk/jspui/bitstream/123456789/877/1/1899S.pdf

[92] Abdul Manan Bazai, "An Assessment of Pak-Afghan Relations, Since 1947 Up to 2001," *University of Balochistan*, 2008, p 177 http://prr.hec.gov.pk/jspui/bitstream/123456789/877/1/1899S.pdf

largely responsible for the creation of the Taliban. It was for economic reasons that the Islamabad was eager to open trade routes to Central Asia. In order to achieve their economic goals, the Pakistani military and the Inter-Services Intelligence agency (ISI) created the Taliban in Afghanistan. There was an unending civil war in Afghanistan that frustrated Pakistani plans. The Taliban movement was supported by Pakistan since its inception, and their weaponry, funding, and training indicated that this was beyond a religious student movement.[93]

The Taliban force was said to contain Pakistani soldiers, according to reports. For instance, Mazar-e-Sharif refugees said that Pakistani fighters who were affiliated with the Taliban were present, as evidenced by their language, dress and use of the flag of a Pakistani Muslim fundamentalist organisation.

The assertion that Interior Minister General (retired) Naseerullah Babar supported the group during Benazir Bhutto's second time in government (1993–1996) was also backed by Pakistani writer Ahmed Rashid. He said that when the Taliban launched its first significant military offensive in October 1994, it purportedly did so with the assistance of Pakistani trucking cartels operating in Chaman and Quetta, close to the Afghan border.[94]

There are also some other reasons in which Pakistan backed the Afghan Taliban. Pakistan desired a peaceful, stable Afghanistan with a cooperative Kabul administration that could, on the one hand, make it easier for the more than 3 million Afghan refugees to return home and, on the other side, offer secure access

---

[93] William Maley, "Afghanistan and the Taliban: The Rebirth of Fundamentalism?, New York University Press, 1998, p. 43-47

[94] Ahmed Rashid, Jihad the Rise of Militant Islam in Central Asia, op.cit., 184.

to Central Asian markets. Gaining "strategic depth" in Afghanistan for the possibility of future conflict with its arch-enemy India was another reason. Since the security of any state is a top priority in the global politics, the Pakistani military essentially feels that it is in the greater national interest of the nation to adopt such measures from a realist viewpoint to lessen the security threat from India.

There is no doubt that Pakistan did not support the Taliban for any ideological reasons. It was founded on strictly geostrategic considerations and attempted to use a Pashtun movement to assert Pakistan's control over Afghanistan. The fundamental goal was to develop strategic depth with respect to India. Military planners in Pakistan felt that a friendly, Pashtun-dominated administration in Afghanistan may provide their nation with a tactical edge over India.[95] Hamid Gul, a former head of Pakistan's powerful military intelligence, also holds the view that Pakistan must pursue strategic depth in Afghanistan for reasons of security.

Meanwhile, Hamid Mir, a senior Pakistani journalist, revealed in his article, “I was invited by the then federal interior minister, Major General Naseerullah Khan Babar, for lunch. He tried to convince me that all patriotic journalists must support the Taliban because they were protecting the economic interests of Pakistan. What was that economic interest? Babar told me that Afghanistan was a gateway to Central Asia and Iran was trying to close this gate for us through the Northern Alliance for its own interest. Further, he said Pakistan was trying to control Afghanistan with the help of the Taliban, and we were heading towards a gas pipeline project from Turkmenistan to Pakistan via Afghanistan worth billions

---

[95] Zahid Hussain, "Frontline Pakistan the Struggle with Militant Islam," Vanguard Books, 2007

of dollars."[96]

Although the contribution Pakistan made to the formation of the Taliban has been widely debated, both sides agreed that Pakistan was the Taliban's main sponsor.

Even though the Taliban controlled nearly 90% of the region, they were only able to convince three nations—Pakistan, United Arab Emirates (UAE) and Saudi Arabia—to recognize them, and the rest of the world refused to acknowledge them.

In terms of foreign policy, the Taliban regime was unable to gain international recognition due to its close ties to several groups that were either designated terrorist organisations or wanted in various states, its ties to Osama Bin Laden, who was staying in Afghanistan and the most wanted person by the USA. Al Qaeda is being one of the major militant groups which has changes the Afghan political system.

Dr Abdullah Azzam, a Palestinian, and a group of spiritual leaders founded Maktaba al Khidmat in Peshawar in 1982. Azzam's assistant was Osama Bin Ladin. The organization's primary goals were to help the Afghan Mujahedeen in many ways, both financially and intellectually. Osama's family provided the majority of the funding because he was a member of an elite family. It should be known that this did not take place in secret and that the CIA and ISI actively supported and assisted them.

However, in the mid-1980s, Osama began to argue with his mentor, Dr Abdullah Azzam. Instead of giving to the cause, Osama Bin Ladin wants to fight in the ground and become a Mujahidin. Osama bin Laden assembled his

---

[96] Hamid Mir, "Afghanistan's pipeline police", September 17, 2002. http://www.rediff.com/news/2002/sep/17guest.htm (accessed on January 18, 2012)

squad of Arab fighters. Initially, the name "Arab Brigade" was popular. Soon after, Osama met Egyptian medical doctor Ayman al Zawahiri, who was treating mujahedeen in Peshawar. Both have the same ideology.

Osama bin Laden founded Al-Qaeda in 1988. Dr Abdullah Azzam used the phrase Al-Qaeda al sulbah in an essay for Jihad magazine in April 1988. Throughout his paper, he emphasises the concept of forming an organisation to provide social services in the Muslim world. He never mentioned his notion in a military context in his article. Osama adopted Azzam's suggestion and founded Al-Qaeda, omitting "Al sulbah." Abdullah Azzam was assassinated a year later and it was assumed that Osama was responsible.[97]

After the Taliban gained control of Afghanistan in 1996, Osama landed in Jalalabad. Arabs from numerous nations who fled following the Afghan Jihad began to return to join Osama. Pakistan and Saudi Arabia also asked the group to hand up Laden for trial, but the Taliban refused. In 1999, the Security Council in its resolution 1267 imposed economic sanctions on Afghanistan.[98]

It is also fact that the US first supported the Afghan Taliban phenomenon because they believed they might help bring stability and peace to Afghanistan. However, the presence of Osama bin Laden and his supporters was causing unrest throughout the West, especially in the US. Although American attitude toward the Taliban was initially unspecific, the August 1998 bombings of two US embassies in Kenya (Nairobi) and Tanzania (Dar es Salaam) caused a change in the course of

---

[97] "Al-Qaeda and Osama bin Laden," *Daily Outlook Afghanistan*, July 06, 2020
http://outlookafghanistan.net/topics.php?post_id=26928

[98] "The situation in Afghanistan," *United Nations*, 1999
http://unscr.com/en/resolutions/doc/1267

events. Because bin Laden and his AL- Qaeda group were held responsible for the assaults, it turned America against the Taliban. But according to the Taliban leadership, there was no proof that Bin Laden was behind such efforts. Osama was designated a terrorist by the US government. The US fired cruise missiles into Afghanistan on August 20, 1998, in retaliation for the country's alleged support of terrorism. As part of their demand for Osama bin Laden's extradition, the US also requested Pakistan to exert influence on Kabul, but Pakistan responded that Washington should speak with Kabul directly.[99]

After providing complete support to the Taliban, Pakistan began to be disappointed by the Taliban when its efforts to moderate policies on socio-cultural concerns, as well as the removal of the Buddha monument, failed. One of the most heinous acts committed by the Taliban was the destruction of two famous Buddha statues in Bamiyan, which had stood for generations. The entire world was looking to Pakistan to persuade the Taliban not to destroy those sculptures, but the Taliban did not listen and smashed them. The Taliban also did not recognize the Durand Line and the policy remain same. They also refused Pakistan's plea to not offer asylum to Pakistanis participating in terrorist actions in Pakistan, claiming that there were no such persons in Afghanistan.

2.3 PAKISTAN-AFGHANISTAN RELATIONS AFTER 9/11

For the discussion of Afghanistan's future, the UN organised the Bonn Conference. It was decided to establish an Afghan interim administration headed by Hamid Karzai with a six-month term beginning on

---

[99] "Taliban and Mullah Omar," *Daily Lead Pakistan*, July 12, 2020 https://leadpakistan.com.pk/news/taliban-and-mullah-omar/

December 22, 2001. Pakistan backed the interim system. Pakistan provided a variety of moral, political and financial support to fortify the newly installed Karzai administration in Kabul.

Delegations to the Loya Jirga were elected in Kabul from June 13 to June 16, 2002. King Zahir Shah had returned to the land and was awarded the position of nominal ruler. However, he declined any position and Hamid Karzai was elected as Head of State. Afghanistan's new president was Hamid Karzai. While the Taliban were dispersed around the country. The United States was likewise under the impression that it would accomplish significant results within a few months. While Karzai was more oriented towards India, New Delhi also discovered a large platform in Afghanistan to launch covert operations in Balochistan and FATA.

Pakistan helps the US with logistics. Military bases in Pasni, Jacobabad, Shamsi and Dalbandin were also given by Pakistan to the US. The soldiers of the alliance received full technical and human intelligence support. Several times, President Pervez Musharraf promised US President George Bush Islamabad's unwavering assistance in the war on terrorism. Pakistan reaffirmed that it will not permit anyone to exploit its territory to undermine Afghanistan.

Pakistan has made more contributions to the US campaign against al Qaeda than any other country, according to Gen. Abizaid, the head of the US Central Command, in January 2004. The US later recognised Pakistan as a crucial ally and promoted it to a "major non-NATO partner" in June 2004.[100]

However, there was still a lack of confidence since the US and the Kabul administration thought Pakistan was

---

[100] K. Alan Kronstadt, "Terrorism in South Asia," CRS Report for Congress, 2004.

giving terrorists a safe haven. In 2004, Colin Powel, the then-secretary of state of the United States, paid a quick visit to Islamabad and informed Musharraf's government that in the event that Pakistan failed to strike the Al-Qaeda terrorists stationed in South Waziristan, the United States would attack South Waziristan. The Musharaf regime began military operations in FATA in response to a US threat. Due to this approach, President Musharraf has repeatedly come under fire in Pakistan for providing too much assistance and concession to the US without any reward.

Along the border with Afghanistan, Pakistan also stationed a large number of soldiers. On the other side, the Taliban and al Qaeda fighters have been able to reassemble in the tribal regions between Afghanistan and Pakistan. Pakistan has been successful in assassinating and seizing a number of key Taliban and al Qaeda commanders during their campaign against terrorist organisations.

Pakistan's influence in Afghanistan has reduced as a result of a significant change in its foreign policy. The Pakistani government has expressed its strong displeasure about India's actions and initiatives near the Pakistan-Afghanistan border in public, which has caused great concern in Islamabad. India was accused of creating fake Pakistani currency and carrying out terrorist and destructive actions within Pakistan. The government of Pakistan alleges attempts to destabilise Pakistan's western provinces, notably the tribal regions of Khyber Pakhtunkhwa and Baluchistan.

According to Mushahid Hussain, the former chair of the Senate Standing Committee on Foreign Affairs claimed in July 2006, nearly 600 Baluchs were being trained by RAW in Afghanistan. He added that RAW had been in contact with Afghan intelligence services and that India was funding the Baloch rebellion.[101]

The Afghan government has often accused Pakistan of aiding and abetting the Taliban in order to demonstrate its power and indispensable status. Pakistan was accused that Islamabad provide safe haven for the Afghan Taliban. While it is no hidden secret that the majority of the senior Taliban leaders were living in Pakistan different cities. The Quetta Shura was also very active.[102]

There are a number of factors to blame for the deterioration in US-Pakistan ties. Attacks using drones are one of them. The airspace of Pakistan was repeatedly violated by drones. US authorities claim that President Musharraf and US officials had a secret agreement at the time in June 2008 to permit US drone operations in Pakistan where terrorists are suspected.[103]

On September 11, 2001, two twin towers of the World Trade Center in New York and the Pentagon Building in Washington were attacked by planes hijacked by suicide bombers. As a result, thousands of people died and the World Trade Center was destroyed, changing the world and causing Pakistan to find itself trapped between the devil and the deep sea. It marks the beginning of a new phase in Pakistan's foreign policy and Afghanistan policy, in particular. America offered Pakistan a stark

---

[101] Frédéric Grare, "Pakistan-Afghanistan relations in the post-9/11 era," Carnegie Papers, 2006, p. 17 https://carnegieendowment.org/files/cp72_grare_final.pdf

[102] Abubakar Siddique, "The Quetta Shura: Understanding the Afghan Taliban's Leadership," *James Foundation*, February 21, 2014 https://jamestown.org/program/the-quetta-shura-understanding-the-afghan-talibans-leadership/

[103] "Suspected U.S. Missile Strike Kills 18 in Pakistan", *Associated Press*, January 23, 2009.

choice; either to be with us or against us.[104]

President of the United States George W. Bush during his famous speech made it clear that “We will starve terrorists of funding, turn them one against another, drive them from place to place until there is no refuge or no rest. And we will pursue nations that provide aid or a safe haven to terrorism. Every nation, in every region, now has the decision to make. Either you are with us, or you are with the terrorists. From this day forward, any nation that continues to harbour or support terrorism will be regarded by the United States as a hostile regime”[105]

Following the Taliban's failure to surrender Bin Ladin to the US on October 7, 2001, the US began its massive carpet-bombing campaign in Afghanistan. In guerilla warfare, Taliban commanders found refuge in rural villages and mountains. Pakistani delegation also visits Kabul to request the Taliban to hand over Osama to the US but the Taliban didn't listen. According to former CIA director George Tenet, Pakistan assisted in setting up talks between Mullah Akhter Mohammed Osmani, the Taliban leader and Robert Grenier, the CIA's Islamabad bureau chief, in order to find a diplomatic resolution.[106] The US and its allies seized control of major cities, including the capital Kabul, within a few weeks. As a result of the Taliban's fall, foreign actors were able to intervene in Afghanistan.

Mullah Omar, the head of the Taliban, fled on a Honda motorbike and disappeared. Prime Minister Koizumi of

---

[104] Pervez Musharraf, "In the Line of fire," *Simon & Schuster,* 2006, p. 201

[105] "Text: President Bush Addresses the Nation," *The Washington Post*, Sept, 20, 2001 https://www.washingtonpost.com/wp-srv/nation/specials/attacked/transcripts/bushaddress_092001.html

[106] George Tenet, "At the Center of the Storm: My Years at the CIA, (New York," Harper Collins, 2007, 182-183

Japan once asked General Musharraf about Mullah Omar. General Musharraf informed him that Omar had fled on a Honda and added light heartedly that the ideal advertisement for Honda would be a commercial showing Omar escaping on one of its motorcycles with his robes and beard blowing in the wind.[107]

At that point, Pakistan has two options: support the US in its fight against Al-Qaeda and the Taliban, or face superpower reprisal if it maintains its pro-Taliban stance. Pakistan has chosen to leave the Taliban behind and join the alliance led by the US. Pakistan's approach toward the Taliban has remained complicated and contradictory. It is also true that Pakistan lost some Pushtun support by withdrawing its backing for the Taliban administration. Later, the West criticised Pakistan's stance, demanding that it "do more" and accusing Pakistan of helping the Taliban. The United States has criticised Pakistan for not doing enough to confront the Taliban, which has caused a rift between Pakistan and the US. However, Pakistan is still directly affected by the economic, strategic as well as political ramifications of the Afghanistan issue.

The terrorist attacks on September 11th, 2001 in the United States had a huge impact on Pakistan. Pakistan initiated military operations against Taliban and Al Qaeda terrorists in its border areas as part of its attempts to help the US-led fight on terror. These operations caused substantial human casualties and population migration, as well as a worsening in Pakistan-Afghanistan relations. The majority of the terrorist attacks and suicide bombings that have targeted the country have been claimed by militant group, like Tehreek e Taliban Pakistan (TTP), often known as the Pakistani Taliban, as well as other

---

[107] Pervez Musharraf, "In the Line of fire," *Simon & Schuster*, 2006

religious extremist organisations. Additionally, this has led to several civilian and security personnel fatalities and injuries. The economy of Pakistan was significantly impacted by the fight against terrorism. Rising unemployment, high inflation and a drop in foreign investment have all been problems for the country. Additionally, the conflict caused a substantial migration of Afghan refugees into Pakistan, straining its resources. Political crises have occurred often in the nation, including the assassination of former prime minister Benazir Bhutto. The general stability of the nation has been negatively impacted by these occurrences, which have worsened political instability.

Pakistan let the US and NATO use Pakistani supply channels for around 75% of their petrol, food and military equipment needs for logistical assistance through the road. This supply channel was crucial to the success of the operations in Afghanistan, but tribal insurgents damaged or destroyed several of them.[108]

As a result of the US invasion of Afghanistan, there were several new militant groups emerged in Pakistan such as Tehreek-e-Taliban Pakistan (TTP). We will discuss TTP in detail in Chapter no 5. In 2002, Pakistan banned religious militant organisations and took action to stop their emergence under false pretences and the solicitation of unrestricted contributions for their operations. The Pakistani government has blacklisted the following organisations: Lashkar-e-Jhangvi, Sipah-e-Muhammad, Sipah-e-Sahaba, TJP, Tehrik-e-Nifaz-e-Shariat Muhammadi (TNSM), Jaish-e-Muhammad and

---

[108] "Pakistan's Role in Global War on Terrorism: and Areas of Clash with United States," *Pakistan Defence,* http://www.defence.pk/forums/strategic-geopoliticalissues/29111-pakistan-s-role-global-war-terrorism-areas-clash-united-states.html (accessed Januray 20, 2022)

Lashkar-e-Taiba.[109]

Pakistan launched several operations in response to militant activity in the Federally Administered Tribal Areas (FATA), including the Al-Mizan Operation (The Balance) in South Waziristan in 2001–2002, the Sherdil Operation (Lion-heart) in Bajaur in 2007, the Zalzala Operation (Earthquake) in South Waziristan in 2008, the Rah-e-Haq Operation (The True Path) in Malakand Additionally, there were a few smaller operations against terrorist organisations such Sirat-e-Mustaqeem, Darghalam, Bia-Darghalam, and Kwakhbadesham in the Khyber Agency.

Although Pakistan has often claimed that it has no affiliation with or assistance for terrorist organisations, the truth is far different. Mullah Abdul Ghani Baradar,[110] a senior military leader for the Taliban, was apprehended in Karachi, Pakistan, in a covert joint operation by Pakistani and American intelligence agents. Famous Quetta shura was active in managing the Afghan war from there. Laden, the founder and founding head of the jihadist organisation Al-Qaeda, was assassinated by the US on May 2, 2011, at his base in the Pakistani city of Abbottabad.

Overall, distrust and collaboration were present in the ties between Pakistan and Afghanistan from 2000 to 2011. While factors including cross-border terrorism, militant organisations and Afghan refugees' presence in Pakistan led to tensions between the two countries, efforts to foster peace and stability, economic aid, commerce and counter-narcotics cooperation did bring

---

[109] "Pakistan: Countering Global Terrorism," *Institute of Regional Studies*, Islamabad, 16.

[110] "Secret Joint Raid Captures Taliban's Top Commander," *The New York Times*, 2010 https://www.nytimes.com/2010/02/16/world/asia/16intel.html

them together.

Pakistan has a history of aiding insurgent groups in Afghanistan. However, it is also true that the United States and its allies fail to get any major military success. Taliban insurgents were active in several parts of Afghanistan and corruption was at its peak in Kabul. As things continued to deteriorate, the US ultimately decided to conduct talks with the Afghan Taliban.

CHAPTER 3

DOHA AGREEMENT

After the Al Qaeda attack on the US in 2001, the western troops landed in Afghanistan with the aim to eliminate the Taliban and Al Qaeda. Initially, from 2001 to 2003, the troops were very successful on the ground operations as the member of both groups were fled from Afghanistan however small resistance inside were also taking place. A Marshall Plan for Afghanistan was also announced by President Bush at the Virginia Military Institute in April 2002.[111] Marshall Plan's aim was to provide financial and development support for Afghanistan following the removal of the Taliban government. It focused was also promotion of democracy. There was not any specific amount set but it was just an effort to provide reconstruction and development assistance to the country.[112]

The US turned its attention after the initial success of the war to Iraq and diverted its military and intelligence resources from Afghanistan.

The US ended major combat operations in Afghanistan on May 1, 2003, though Donald Rumsfeld said that "pockets of resistance" remained in some areas. According to Rumsfeld, President Bush, US Central

---

[111] Jeffrey Donovan, "Afghanistan: Bush Likens U.S. Effort To Marshall Plan," *Radio Free Europe/Radio Liberty*, April 2002 https://www.rferl.org/a/1099500.html

[112] Ibid

Command Chief Gen. Tommy Franks and Afghan President Karzai "have concluded that we have moved from a period of major combat activity to one of stability, stabilization and reconstruction."[113] While during this era the US send more troops to Afghanistan.

The Taliban had begun to reorganize their forces in the eastern and southern regions of the country by 2005. In 2006, Taliban forces were reportedly clashing daily with US and coalition forces and governing areas of southern Afghanistan.[114] Although NATO forces reduced Taliban control in the south and east, they did not eliminate it.

In rural and remote areas, the Taliban gradually regained control of parts of the country. Furthermore, they continued to launch bombings and other attacks against government and coalition targets.

As the fighting continued for a long period of time and the number of casualties increased, many Western countries lost their support for the war, putting pressure on the governments to keep the troops safe or remove them from war.

The Afghan security forces began to assume security responsibilities from international forces in mid-2011, as scheduled. These forces were weakened and remained largely dependent on the United States for logistical and tactical support. Meanwhile, the Taliban possessed a large and effective intelligence network and its fighters remained highly motivated.

As a result of effective Taliban operations, which also decreased the Afghan government's own capabilities, the public's trust in the government and its security forces was repeatedly eroded. Meanwhile, the Obama

---

[113] "Rumsfeld: Major combat over in Afghanistan," *CNN*, May 1, 2003.

[114] Carlotta Gall, "Taliban Surges as U.S. Shifts Some Tasks to NATO," *New York Times*, June 11, 2006.

administration came to the conclusion that there was no military way to resolve the conflict and started informal talks with the Taliban in 2010.[115]

The negotiations focused mostly on confidence-building measures, including the establishment of a Taliban political office in Doha, Qatar. The Taliban was not ready to engage with the Afghan government as the Taliban called the Afghan government puppet to the US. Taliban wants to hold direct negotiations with the US. While Afghan government also shows concern to the US that there should be government representatives in the negotiations. Finally, talks ended in 2014 with no result.

On the other hand, there were some other developments which also affect the Pak Afghan relations as well as the US concerns. Bin Laden, the al-Qaeda commander responsible for the 9/11 attacks, was assassinated by US forces in Pakistan in 2011. The death of the United States' top target in a war that began ten years ago intensifies the long-simmering argument about whether or not to continue the war in Afghanistan. Meanwhile, anti-Pakistan rhetoric grows in Afghanistan, where officials have long blamed terrorist safe havens in Pakistan for violence in Afghanistan.

President Obama several times plans to withdraw all combat troops from Afghanistan, but serious doubts remain about the Afghan government's capacity to secure the country.

In 2011, an international conference also takes place regarding Afghanistan in Bonn, Germany, set out to plan the future of the invaded country. Goals were set for the transfer of power in Afghanistan, as well as for security. While the two major parties Taliban who were gaining control again and Pakistan, the key allies of the US,

---

[115] "White House shifts Afghanistan strategy towards talks with Taliban," *Guardian*, July 19, 2010.

were absent from the conference. Pakistan's decision not to attend the Bonn conference was to protest against the NATO cross-border attack that killed 24 Pakistani soldiers. [116] This conference was not much affected because the major two parties were not present.

In 2014, Karzai era ended. While the new elections also lead to new chaos. Ashraf Ghani and Abdullah Abdullah reached an agreement to establish a unity government after months of disagreement on who was the legitimate winner of the run-off presidential election. As part of the agreement, Dr. Ghani will take office as president and Dr. Abdullah will hold the newly created position of chief executive, which is akin to the prime minister.

The year 2015 was also a time of transition for the Taliban as well as the group admitted its founder Mullah Mohammad Omar had died in 2013 and announced Mullah Akhtar Mansour as the group's new leader, amid reports of contention among Taliban leaders about the succession.[117] Akhtar Mansour was killed in a US drone strike in Pakistan in May 2016 and succeeded by Haibatullah Akhundzada, a religious scholar.[118]

When President Donald Trump came to power, the Afghan policy was again shifted to the withdrawal of the troops. It is also the fact that both in Obama's ear and during the Trump administration, initially, they send

---

[116] "Pakistan says decision to boycott Bonn conference is final," *The Express Tribune*, 2011
https://tribune.com.pk/story/300020/pakistan-says-decision-to-boycott-bonn-conference-is-final

[117] Barnett Rubin, "Turmoil in the Taliban," *New Yorker*, July 31, 2015

[118] Mujib Mashal, Taimoor Shah, "Taliban's New Leader, More Scholar Than Fighter, Is Slow to Impose Himself," *The New York Times, 2016*
https://www.nytimes.com/2016/07/12/world/asia/taliban-afghanistan-pakistan-mawlawi-haibatullah-akhundzada.html

more troops to Afghanistan but later their policy was shifted towards the withdrawal. The Trump administration took several initiatives which leads towards the Doha accord. On the other hands, the Taliban was also looking towards talk and several times demanded the US to withdraw the troops. In August 2017, the Taliban released an open letter to President Trump demanding to pull US troops out of Afghanistan. [119] The US war in Afghanistan was considered a failure by Donald Trump and he promised to end it. Almost 11000 American soldiers were present in Afghanistan at the start of the president's tenure, and he gave the order to increase the number of troops in June 2017. He deployed nearly 3500 additional soldiers in September 2017, resulting in an increase of between 1400 and 1500 additional US troops in Afghanistan by the year's end.

Within a year, President Trump became dissatisfied with the lack of military success against the Taliban and for the first time, he ordered officials to hold direct negotiations with the group without Afghan government participation. It also represented a fundamental change in US strategy toward Afghanistan.[120] Zalmay Khalilzad was appointed as the Special Representative for Afghanistan Reconciliation by the US government. He previously served as permanent representative to the United Nations from 2007 to 2009, as ambassador to Iraq from 2005 to 2007 and as ambassador to Afghanistan from 2003 to 2005. In other words, he had vast experience handling Afghanistan.

---

[119] Justin Rowlatt, "Taliban open letter to Trump urges Afghan withdrawal," *BBC*, August 15, 2017

[120] Mujib Mashal, Eric Schmitt, "White House Orders Direct Taliban Talks to Jump-Start Afghan Negotiations," *The New York Times*, 2018 https://www.nytimes.com/2018/07/15/world/asia/afghanistan-taliban-direct-negotiations.html

While during the Afghan conflict, it is also fact that the US had three options. First, continue to fight against the Afghan Taliban for an unspecified period by increasing its military presence. Unfortunately, this option did not prove to be very successful. A second option was to pull out without any agreement, but it was more embarrassing for the US. The third possibility was to hand over Kabul to the Taliban by negotiating a weak agreement in the absence of other major actors. As a result of the 'Doha Agreement,' was negotiated. It could be argued that the US has used the third option in the Afghan conflict. In 2019 Donald Trump directed his aides to reduce US troops.[121]

On February 29, 2020, finally, the US and the Taliban signed an official deal, which helped the US in its troops, non-diplomatic people and contractors withdraw from Afghanistan and a total withdrawal by the end of April 2021. The deal was commonly known as Doha Agreement. The agreement was brokered by the United States and was aimed at ending the ongoing conflict in Afghanistan. Despite the Taliban's agreement not to use Afghan soil against any other nation or provide safe haven to terrorist groups, the agreement did not include any conditions requiring the Taliban to decrease violence in Afghanistan. A decision was also made to begin intra-Afghan talks. In addition, the prisoner exchange was also finalized. However, the intra-Afghan talks started with a deadlock and they did not

---

[121] John Hudson, "Trump directed aides to reduce U.S. troops in Afghanistan by 2020 election, Pompeo says," *The Washington Post,* July 29, 2019 https://www.washingtonpost.com/world/national-security/trump-directed-aides-to-reduce-us-troops-in-afghanistan-by-2020-election-pompeo-says/2019/07/29/5546df7d-d2fd-443f-ae05-e78bab070bad_story.html

succeed.[122]

In January 2021, only a few thousand US troops remained on Afghan soil after President Trump's tenure ended. However, the Afghan government and Taliban failed to make any progress in their peace talks. Doha's deal was essentially based on four terms:

- Security and enforcement mechanisms will prevent anyone from using Afghanistan's land to threaten or harm the USA and its allies.
- The announcement of a timeline for the withdrawal of all foreign forces from Afghanistan, along with assurances and enforcement mechanisms.
- The Taliban and the Afghan government will begin intra-Afghan peace negotiations on March 10th, 2020.
- Intra-Afghan peace negotiations would discuss a permanent ceasefire, the date and shape of the comprehensive ceasefire, including the mechanisms for applying for shares, which would be announced along with a deal on the future political map of Afghanistan.[123]

It is also the fact that Trump was the main cause of the US withdrawal from Afghanistan since he believes that the US didn't benefit much from that invasion rather the US suffered a huge loss and put a bad reputation in the global community. He also promised this during his electoral campaign. The US withdrawal from

---

[122] Gulabudin Ghubar, "Taliban Blames Govt for Delay in Peace Talks," *Tolo News*, July 19, 2020 https://tolonews.com/afghanistan/taliban-blames-govt-delay-peace-talks

[123] "Donald Trump isolationist doctrine “America first”: A case study of the US withdrawal from Afghanistan," *University Mohamed Boudiaf*

Afghanistan consider a tough decision but it leads towards the end of the 20-year war. However, there may be some changes in the interest of the US as the destabilise South Asian region is more favourable for the US as the influence of China is increasing but, in the end, the US have to end this longstanding war.

A month after the Doha accord, US officials accused Taliban of not fulfilling their obligations under it, especially with regard to Al Qaeda.[124] Also, they said the Taliban's increased violence was "not compatible" with the accord.[125] While the Taliban were prominently active in attacking Afghan security forces but they committed not to attack US forces.[126] No US forces were killed in Afghanistan by Taliban forces after February 2020 however casualties among Afghan military forces and civilians remained high.[127]

The Biden administration began with a promise to perform better than the Trump administration. They also allude to reviewing the agreement, including the Taliban's commitment to it, with the belief that the organisation would "carry the repercussions of its choices" if it fails to hold promise. Before the February 2020 deal, the US began reducing forces and continued to do so later, reaching a low of 2,500 by the time President Trump left office in January 2021.[128]

Following an administration review of US policy in

---

[124] "Taliban not living up to its commitments, U.S. Defense Secretary says," *Reuters,* May 5, 2020.

[125] "Violence 'Not Consistent' with US-Taliban Deal: US Envoy," *TOLOnews,* October 13, 2020.

[126] "Senate Armed Services Committee Holds Hearing on the Defense Budget Posture," CQ, March 4, 2020.

[127] Marvin Weinbaum, "The Taliban's two-track strategy," *Middle East Institute,* June 8, 2020.

[128] "U.S. Is Quietly Reducing Its Troop Force in Afghanistan," *New York Times*, October 21, 2019.

Afghanistan, President Biden announced on April 14, 2021, that while the US-Taliban agreement was "perhaps not what I would have negotiated myself," the US would stick to it by beginning a "final withdrawal" on May 1, 2021, with a goal of completing it by September 11, 2021.[129] The deadline was, however, repeatedly missed by the US side due to the no progress in the discussions. The Taliban however, maintained to refrain from striking US soldiers while accusing the US of breaking the deal by extending it.[130]

The Doha agreement was seen as a significant step towards peace in Afghanistan, as it marked the first time the Taliban had also agreed to hold talks with the Afghan government too. However, it was also met with criticism from some quarters, who felt that the agreement did not go far enough in addressing the root causes of the conflict, and would not lead to lasting peace.

One of the key criticisms of the Doha Agreement is that it did not address the issue of power-sharing between the Taliban and the Afghan government. The agreement called for the release of 5,000 Taliban prisoners but did not address the issue of how the Taliban would be integrated into the Afghan government. Some analysts argued that without a clear plan for power-sharing, the agreement would simply pave the way for the Taliban to take over the government once again.

The United States start negotiations with the Taliban because of the long-lasting war in Afghanistan and the lack of progress in the war effort. The US government saw the Taliban as a key player in the conflict and believed that engaging in direct talks with the group was necessary in order to bring about lasting peace.

---

[129] White House, "Remarks by President Biden on the Way Forward in Afghanistan," April 14, 2021.

[130] "Statement of Islamic Emirate regarding recent announcement by US President Joe Biden," *Voice of Jihad,* April 15, 2021.

Additionally, the US government was looking to withdraw its troops from Afghanistan and believed that a peace agreement with the Taliban would be the best way to accomplish this goal.

Another reason why the US started negotiations with the Taliban is that they believed the Taliban was the only group that had the power to bring stability to Afghanistan, which was in the interest of the US. The Taliban controlled large parts of the country and had a strong influence on the local population. The US government believed that engaging with the group would be the best way to bring about lasting peace in the country.

Pakistan played a significant role in the negotiations leading up to the Doha Agreement. Pakistan has long been accused of supporting the Taliban and has also been accused as a major spoiler in the peace process. However, Pakistan also has a vested interest in a stable Afghanistan, as instability in the country has led to a spill over of violence and extremism into Pakistan.

Pakistan's role in the negotiations was also controversial. Some experts praised Pakistan for its efforts to bring the Taliban to the negotiating table, while others criticized the country for not doing enough to pressure the Taliban to accept a power-sharing agreement with the Afghan government. Pakistan played a key role in the release of Taliban prisoners, which was one of the key demands of the Taliban before they would agree to negotiations. Pakistan was also seen as playing a mediating role between the US and the Taliban. Pakistan's role in the negotiations has been criticized for being too focused on short-term gains rather than long-term stability in the region.

According to former Afghan leaders and some US and Western officials, the Taliban's existence—and its strength and endurance over the past two decades—is due to Pakistan's military and intelligence services' active or passive support, including allowing them to maintain safe havens on Pakistani soil.[131]

Pakistan provided support to the Trump Administration in facilitating US talks with the Taliban after 2018 and US assessments of Pakistan's role in this process have generally been positive.[132] Pakistan hailed the US-Taliban agreement from February 2020 as a validation of its "long-held belief that there is no military solution to the Afghan war" and said it would open the door for intra-Afghan discussions.[133]

A trillion dollars was spent on direct costs by the US, 2,501 people died, and more than 20,000 were wounded in the Afghan war.[134] With the elimination of bin Laden and the reduction of terrorist threats from Afghanistan, Biden believes that the goals of the war have been achieved, so American troops no longer need to be present on the ground. As far as Afghanistan was concerned, Biden supported his approach by citing the many years that the United States and its allies had provided aid.[135]

---

[131] "Some Afghans Blame Neighboring Pakistan for Taliban Gains," *Associated Press*, August 12, 2021

[132] "Mullah Baradar released by Pakistan at the behest of US: Khalilzad," *The Hindu,* February 9, 2019

[133] "Afghan Study Group Final Report: A Pathway for Peace in Afghanistan," *US Institute of Peace*, February 3, 2021

[134] "Remarks by President Biden on the Way Forward in Afghanistan," *The White House*, April 14, 2021 https://www.whitehouse.gov/briefing-room/speeches-remarks/2021/04/14/remarks-by-president-biden-on-the-way-forward-in-afghanistan/

[135] "Remarks by President Biden on the Way Forward in Afghanistan," *The White House*, April 14, 2021 https://www.whitehouse.gov/briefing-room/speeches-remarks/2021/04/14/remarks-by-president-biden-on-the-way-forward-in-afghanistan/

US officials declared the end of the military and diplomatic staff's departure from Afghanistan on August 30, 2021, and they also said that they had essentially finished their airlifting operations for American nationals, lawful permanent residents (LPRs) and some Afghans. According to the State Department and the Military, they directly evacuated or assisted in the evacuation of over 124,000 people, including around 6,000 Americans.[136]

President Biden has praised the operation as an "extraordinary success," although around 100 American citizens and thousands of eligible Afghans remain in Afghanistan, many of whom want to leave.[137]

Several Congressmen and rescue organisations have cast doubt on this number, claiming that there may be hundreds more Americans in Afghanistan than the Government has estimated.[138]

According to President Biden, the United States is still committed to helping eligible individuals, including American citizens, who want to leave Afghanistan. He also pledged to keep the Taliban accountable for their promise to guarantee safe passage.[139]

Meanwhile, China and Russia expressed concern about the consequences of the US withdrawal. The US

---

[136] US Department of Defense, "Secretary of Defense Austin and Chairman of the Joint Chiefs of Staff Gen. Milley Press Briefing," September 1, 2021.

[137] "Remarks by President Biden on the End of the War in Afghanistan," https://www.whitehouse.gov/briefing-room/speeches-remarks/2021/08/31/remarks-by-president-biden-on-the-end-of-the-war-in-afghanistan/

[138] Julie Watson and Bernard Condon, "Rescue groups: US tally misses hundreds left in Afghanistan," *Associated Press,* September 4, 2021.

[139] The White House, "Remarks by President Biden on the End of the War in Afghanistan," August 31, 2021.

extension was earlier referred to by Russia as a violation of the withdrawal agreement by May 1, but it also found concerns that the armed conflict in Afghanistan might escalate in the near future, which could undermine efforts to begin direct intra-Afghan negotiations. Both Russia and China were concerned that the rapid withdrawal would result in instability and give terrorists more room to operate.[140]

While, the Doha Agreement was a significant step towards peace in Afghanistan but was also met with criticism from some quarters. Some key criticisms include that the agreement did not address the problems of power-sharing between the Afghan government and Taliban and did not include the participation of other major actors in the region. The United States began negotiating with the Taliban to bring about lasting peace in Afghanistan and to withdraw its troops from the country.

3.1 SECOND PHASE OF TALIBAN

In its 2021 annual threat assessment, the Office of the Director of National Intelligence stated that "the Afghan Government will struggle to hold the Taliban at bay if the Coalition withdraws support." [141] An external assessment published in January 2021 concluded that the Taliban enjoyed a strong advantage over the Afghanistan National Defense and Security Forces (ANDSF) in cohesion and a slight advantage in force

---

[140] Russia says US plan for troop pullout from Afghanistan risks 'escalation,' *Al Arabiya News,* https://english.alarabiya.net/News/world/2021/04/14/Russia-says-US-plan-for-troop-pullout-from-Afghanistan-risks-escalation-

[141] "Annual Threat Assessment of the U.S. Intelligence Community, Office of the Director of National Intelligence," April 09, 2021 https://www.dni.gov/files/ODNI/documents/assessments/ATA-2021-Unclassified-Report.pdf

employment and that the two forces essentially split on material resources and external support.[142]

By early May 2021, the Taliban had captured large swaths of rural parts of Afghanistan, securing their hold on some areas they already occupied. It was more surprising that the Taliban seized other districts than the southern ones: some northern areas had militarily resisted them during the Taliban's rule in the 1990s, making their fall to the Taliban in 2021 a significant event. As of May, and June 2021, over 100 of Afghanistan's 400 districts were under Taliban control.[143]

Despite the Taliban's rapid advance, some within the group claimed they were deliberately avoiding capturing province capitals prior to US departure.[144] In July, the Taliban began seizing border crossings with Tajikistan, Iran and Pakistan. The Taliban captured Zaranj on August 6, 2021. Observers and US officials were shocked when the Taliban captured half of Afghanistan's provincial capitals in the following week.[145]

After Jalalabad in the east and Mazar-e-Sharif in the north fell, the Taliban seized the remaining significant cities and vanquished the last strongholds of the organised Afghan government opposition.

---

[142] Jonathan Schroden, "Afghanistan Security Forces Versus the Taliban: A Net Assessment," CTC Sentinel, Vol. 14, Issue 1, January 2021.

[143] Kate Clark, Obaid Ali, "A Quarter of Afghanistan's Districts Fall to the Taleban amid Calls for a 'Second Resistance,'" Afghanistan Analysts Network, July 2, 2021.

[144] Dan De Luce, Mushtaq Yusufzai, and Saphora Smith, "Even the Taliban are surprised at how fast they're advancing in Afghanistan," *NBC News*, June 25, 2021.

[145] Zeke Miller et al., "Biden team surprised by rapid Taliban gains in Afghanistan," *Associated Press*, August 15, 2021.

The Taliban officially took over the country on August 15, 2021, when they started moving into Kabul. In September 2021, Taliban troops are said to have taken control of the central province of Panjshir, where some former Afghan officials sought to organise armed opposition to the Taliban.[146]

Following the Taliban takeover, US officials told Senators in August 2021 that "terror groups like al-Qaeda may be able to grow much faster than expected".[147]

In September 2021, US intelligence officials reportedly stated that Al Qaeda could "build some capability to threaten the homeland" within a year or two.[148] AQ supporters were reported to have greeted the Taliban takeover in Afghanistan as a victory for global jihadism, which might expand beyond Afghanistan.

Ashraf Ghani fled the country on August 15, 2021, after a seven-year tenure characterized by electoral crisis, faction infighting and the gradual weakening of Afghan forces. Ghani said in a statement that he left Kabul to prevent bloodshed and that the Taliban had won the sword and gun judgment and now they must protect the honour, wealth and self-esteem of the Afghan people.[149]

---

[146] "Afghanistan crisis: Taliban kill civilians in resistance stronghold," *BBC*, September 13, 2021.

[147] "Concerns over US terror threat rising as Taliban hold grows," Associated Press, August 15, 2021. https://apnews.com/article/joe-biden-taliban-ffa2ce2739f5be13e73db65c4a93cd54

[148] "Al Qaeda Could Rebuilt in Afghanistan in a Year or Two, US Officials Say," *New York Times*, September 14, 2021.

[149] Chantal Da Silva, Ahmed Mengli and Mushtaq Yusufzai, "From Afghan nation-builder to life in 'exile': Ashraf Ghani flees country in defeat," *NBC News,* August 16, 2021. https://www.nbcnews.com/news/world/afghan-nationbuilder-life-exile-ashraf-ghani-flees-country-defeat-n1276826

The Ministry of Foreign Affairs and International Cooperation of the United Arab Emirates (UAE) announced on August 18 that "the UAE has welcomed President Ashraf Ghani and his family into the country on humanitarian grounds" after days of inquiries about his whereabouts.[150]

Besides government-aligned elites, many other influential powerbrokers have left or been side-lined by the takeover. The Taliban captured former Herat governor Ismail Khan during fighting in Herat, but he was allowed to move to Iran after being captured by them.[151] In the northern city of Mazar-e-Sharif, Marshal Abdul Rashid Dostum and Atta Mohammad Noor gathered their forces and fled to Uzbekistan.[152]

Taliban spokesperson Zabihullah Mujahid makes his first public appearance on September 7, 2021. He released the names of 33 “acting” ministers who will serve in a “caretaker cabinet” to manage the country. The Taliban refer to this administration as the Islamic Emirate of Afghanistan.[153]

As the Taliban’s emir, Haibatullah Akhundzada holds absolute control. Mohammad Hassan Akhund, the former governor of Kandahar and foreign minister in the Taliban regime of the 1990s, has been appointed as

---

[150] “UAE Ministry of Foreign Affairs and International Cooperation, Statement on President Ashraf Ghani,” August 18 2021.

[151] Mac Caltrider, "UPDATE: ‘LION OF HERAT’ REPORTEDLY IN IRAN FOLLOWING TALIBAN CAPTURE," *Coffee or Die,* August 19, 2021 https://coffeeordie.com/ismail-khan-herat-iran

[152] "Afghan militia leaders Atta Noor, Dostum escape 'conspiracy'," *Reuters,* August 15, 2021 https://www.reuters.com/world/asia-pacific/afghan-militia-leaders-atta-noor-dostum-escape-conspiracy-2021-08-14/

[153] “Who Will Run the Taliban Government?” *International Crisis Group*, September 9, 2021.

Interim Prime Minister.[154]

The discussions with the United States were led by Abdul Ghani Baradar, who was later appointed acting deputy prime minister. On September 13, 2021, Baradar made an audio recording denying rumours that he had been killed or injured in a fight with other Taliban leaders. The BBC reported on September 15, 2021, that Baradar had left for Kandahar after a heated disagreement with Haqqani leaders over whether the Taliban's political or military wings should be given credit for the group's takeover.[155]

Taliban officials have met with Afghan political leaders after the group took over, including Abdullah Abdullah, former President Hamid Karzai, and former Islamist insurgent leader Gulbuddin Hekmatyar. However, they do not serve in the Taliban government. Karzai and Abdullah were described as being “effectively under house arrest” by the media on August 26.[156]

The vast bulk of the Taliban caretaker government is either former Taliban leaders or passionate Taliban loyalists. All of the "caretaker cabinet" members are male, with the majority of them being ethnic Pashtuns from southern Afghanistan. The majority of them have previously been the subject of US or UN sanctions, including the acting interior minister, Sirajuddin Haqqani. The US Department of State also announced a reward of up to $10 million for information that helps in the capture of Haqqani, the leader of the Haqqani Network.

---

[154] Martine van Bijlert, “The Focus of the Taleban’s New Government: Internal cohesion, external dominance,” *Afghanistan Analysts Network*, September 12, 2021.

[155] Khudai Noor Nasar, “Afghanistan: Taliban leaders in bust-up at presidential palace, sources say,” *BBC,* September 15, 2021.

[156] Nic Robertson, “Taliban removes security from ex-Afghan President Hamid Karzai and Abdullah Abdullah, source says,” *CNN*, August 26, 2021.

Neither the United States nor the rest of the global community recognised the Afghan Taliban regime as the legitimate government of Afghanistan when it seized power in Afghanistan in 1996 and served as the de facto government up until the US invasion in 2001. Saudi Arabia, the United Arab Emirates and Pakistan were the only three countries that have formally recognised the Taliban. The question of whether the Taliban should represent Afghanistan or the Permanent Representative of Afghanistan at the UN was postponed indefinitely by the UN General Assembly's Credentials Committee.

The Taliban were "not recognised at the United Nations and moreover, the Security Council does not support the reinstatement of the Islamic Emirate of Afghanistan," according to UN Security Council Resolution 2513[157]. Taliban are still facing international reorganization from international community as the world are demanding do more from the group.

Although the Taliban quickly took control in August 2021, this was not because they enjoyed strong popular support; rather, it was because the previous administration clearly had very limited support. The Doha agreement played a significant role while ending the long-standing 20 years of war. The US withdrew its troops while Kabul goes to the hand of the Taliban. The Taliban did several commitments which will take some time to fulfilling it.

---

[157] "The situation in Afghanistan," *United Nations*, 2020 http://unscr.com/en/resolutions/doc/2513

CHAPTER 4

EXPLORING PAK-AFGHAN RELATIONS: ADDRESSING CHALLENGES, UNVEILING OPPORTUNITIES AND CHARTING A PATH FOR ENHANCED ENGAGEMENT

Afghanistan has long been a critical country in the region and changes in its political, social and economic landscape have had significant implications for the entire Central Asian region, including Pakistan. With the Taliban taking over Afghanistan after 20 years of insurgency, the region has undergone significant changes. As there are several challenges for Pakistan after the re-emergence of Afghan Taliban, there are also some opportunities which will boost the relations between the two nations to cooperate in the diverse field. The following discussion contemplate on challenges and opportunities and a way forward for Pakistan.

4.1 CHALLENGES

Overall, the re-emergence of the Afghan Taliban is a complex issue that poses multifaceted challenges to Pakistan's security, economy, and social fabric. The following are the major challenges for Pakistan.

1) Security Threats

Pakistan has been grappling with security threats for decades. The country has witnessed terrorist activities, insurgency and sectarian violence. One of the significant reasons behind the security threats in Pakistan is the Afghanistan war. Afghan Taliban during the US invasion hide in Pakistan's Tribal region. Tribal people during the war have shown some sympathies for the Afghan Taliban and later on, the new group emerged under the name of Tehreek-e-Taliban Pakistan (TTP). In some section, TTP is considered the proxy of the Afghan Taliban in Pakistan.[158] As a result of the fall of Kabul, the Tehreek-e-Taliban Pakistan (TTP), who killed tens of thousands of Pakistanis from 2007 to 2014, has once again re-emerged and pose a greater threat to Pakistan.[159]

Since the Afghan Taliban came to power in August 2021, the number of terrorist attacks in Pakistan increased by 51 per cent. Between August 15, 2021, and August 14, 2022, a total of 250 assaults in Pakistan—mostly in the northwest—led to the deaths of 433 people and the injuries of 719 others. In contrast, 165 incidents between August 2020 and August 14, 2021, led to the deaths of 294 people and the injuries of 598 others. [160] Moreover, the proscribed Tehreek-e-

---

[158] Roohan Ahmed, Uzair Younus, "With No Help from Kabul, Pakistan Faces the TTP Threat," *New Lines Institute for Strategy and Policy,* January 19, 2023
https://newlinesinstitute.org/pakistan/with-no-help-from-kabul-pakistan-faces-the-ttp-threat/

[159] Abid Hussain, "What is behind a resurgence of violent attacks in Pakistan?," *Al Jazeera*, 26 Dec 2022
https://www.aljazeera.com/news/2022/12/26/what-is-behind-a-resurgence-of-violent-attacks-in-pakistan

[160] Iftikhar A. Khan, "Terror attacks in Pakistan surge by 51pc after Afghan Taliban victory," *DAWN*, October 20, 2022
https://www.dawn.com/news/1715927

Taliban Pakistan (TTP), which is believed to operate from Afghanistan, is causing problems for Islamabad's relations with the Taliban government. According to the Global Terrorism Index, Pakistan has consistently been one of the countries most affected by terrorism and after the fall of Kabul, the situation has gone worst.

While Pakistan has attempted to negotiate with the TTP in the presence of the Afghan Taliban several times, the negotiations have failed each time. The group opposes the notion of the Pakistani state fundamentally. TTP is receiving safe heavens from the Afghan Taliban as they believe TTP helped them settle in Pakistan in their difficult times. Additionally, border classes are increasing. While there is no guarantee that if Pakistan and TTP negotiations are successful the TTP militants who disagree with the decision will never join any other group like ISKP. Over the last few years, the TTP has also been able to regroup and reorganize its fighters, and they are now better trained, more equipped and more ideologically committed than ever.

Other militant groups, such as the Islamic State Khorasan Province (ISKP) and Baloch militants, are also celebrating the Afghan Taliban's success in military causes as an inspiration for them. On the other hand, the ISKP and the Afghan Taliban have ideological differences that have a direct impact on Pakistan's security situation, as several ISKP militants have move to Pakistan. Khyber Pakhtunkhwa's then police chief Moazzam Jah Ansari said that IS-KP, the Khorasan chapter of the Islamic State group, is a more serious threat to the province than the TTP.[161] Meanwhile, Baloch militants have also increased their attacks on Pakistani government officials. TTP has even formalised

---

[161] Manzoor Ali, "KP police chief calls IS-K bigger threat than TTP," *DAWN*, January 21, 2022 https://www.dawn.com/news/1670641

tactical alliances with Baloch rebel groups in Balochistan, further complicating Pakistani security challenges.

Despite most of Pakistan's border with Afghanistan being sealed off, these TTP elements easily cross it, posing a significant challenge to the country. Despite repeated assurances that Afghan land will not be used by militants for activities against other countries, the Afghan Taliban have been unwilling to take a clear position regarding the TTP. It is also fact that previously this tribal region was neglected by many facilities like infractions, education, proper government setup and TTP is now utilizing and highlight the basic needs of people. Meanwhile, TTP has claimed several times that they do not need to operate on Afghan soil because they already control a large portion of tribal areas in Pakistan.

The current wave of terrorism also threats the Chinese interest in Pakistan particularly the multi-billion-dollar China-Pakistan Economic Corridor (CPEC). This project was a game-changer for Pakistan. The project includes the construction of roads, pipelines, railways and other infrastructure projects in Pakistan but due to attacks on chines officials, the progress is slow. Militant attacks in the region have targeted CPEC projects and workers, causing delays and disruptions.

The Taliban takeover has also led to an increase in cross-border terrorism from Afghanistan into Pakistan. Militant groups, including TTP, ISKP have been using the porous border between the two countries to launch attacks on Pakistani targets. The Pakistani military has responded by increasing its presence along the border and launching counter-terrorism operations against militant groups operating in the border region but yet there is no positive response from the Afghan side. Not only TTP is threatening the government departments but they also issued an explicit warning to the political parties and threatened to attack their leadership.[162]

Pakistan earlier believes that with a Taliban takeover in Afghanistan, their western borders will be secured because India will be out of the scene but in reality, Pakistan is facing more security threats from the western border as compared to the eastern one. With the fall of Kabul, security threats have increased in Pakistan and there are very minimal chances of any betterment till the Afghan Taliban take this subject seriously and cooperate with Pakistan.

Senior journalist and expert on Afghan Affairs Tahir Khan said that “Pakistan believes that the biggest issue for Islamabad is the Tehreek-e-Taliban Pakistan (TTP) and for this Pakistan earlier believed that after the Afghan Taliban comes to power in Afghanistan, they will help them to stop TTP activities against Pakistan. Although they did mediation and hosted dialogue but Afghan Taliban said that Pakistan should solve this issue through political means."[163]

“Afghan Taliban can't put pressure on Pakistani Taliban because first TTP pledged allegiance to Afghan Taliban and they have a similar ideology. Secondly, they fight together against NATO and the third reason is that after 9/11 Afghan Taliban were hosted by the TTP,” Tahir Khan added.[164]

Tahir Khan further said that “the security threat increases, refugee crisis also increases after the fall of Kabul. Although, the war is ended but for Pakistan,

---

[162] Abid Hussain, "Pakistan Taliban threatens top political leadership including PM," *Al Jazeera*, 4 January, 2023 https://www.aljazeera.com/news/2023/1/4/pakistan-taliban-threatens-top-political-leadership-including-pm

[163] Tahir Khan, Interview by Author, March 15, 2023.

[164] Ibid

challenges have increased."[165]

"Trust is another biggest challenge for Pakistan as there is some negative impression of Islamabad inside Afghan society. Although Pakistan has great relations with the Afghan Taliban but unfortunately Taliban fails to highlight even Pakistan's positive role," Tahir Khan believes.[166]

Faheem Jeffery, who is the Deputy Director of Islamic Theology of Counter Terrorism (ITCT), a UK-based Counter Islamist Terrorism think tank, also believes that "for Pakistan, Taliban re-emergence has more cons than benefits. The biggest impact which is already started is the security challenges. Taliban is an Islamic group with some colours of nationalism. When I say nationalism its means Pashtoon nationalism. These two are the major component of their ideology. Groups which have a similar ideology like Tehreek e Taliban Pakistan (TTP) have a soft corner from the Afghan Taliban and accept the Taliban as an ideological ally. Other small groups either in Punjab or in Karachi, are also a big threat to Pakistan."[167]

2) Economic Consequences

Not only the return of the Afghan Taliban raises primary security concerns but it is also related to the economic challenges. Currently, there have been a series of economic crises in Pakistan, predating the 2022 summer's catastrophic floods. With inflation at unprecedented levels, the rupee value has plummeted and foreign reserves are at an all-time low, they cannot cover even one month's imports, raising the risks of default.

According to Bloomberg report, $5 million are being

---

[165] Ibid

[166] Ibid

[167] Faheem Jeffery, Interview by Author, March 15, 2023.

smuggled daily from Pakistan to Afghanistan.[168] A squeezed economy is supported by the smuggling of dollars. Although smuggled dollars are the Taliban government's lifeline, they are seriously hurting Pakistan's economy. Since the US withdrawal and the fall of Kabul, Afghanistan's banking system have not been connected to international financial institutions. Afghan central banks, however, have reportedly plenty of dollar reserves despite sanctions and internal turmoil.

Dollar smuggling has been a long-standing issue in Pakistan. One of the major impacts of dollar smuggling is the devaluation of the Pakistani rupee. When dollars are smuggled out of the country, the demand for rupees decreases, which leads to a decline in the value of the Pakistani currency. This, in turn, makes imports more expensive and reduces the purchasing power of the common people. Moreover, dollar smuggling also reduces the country's foreign reserves. So directly, after the re-emergence of the Afghan Taliban, the international banking system is closed for Afghanistan and Pakistan is facing the consequences to fulfil its demand.

Faheem Jeffery said that "the economic dimension is also another challenge as the smuggling of dollars is at its peak."[169]

Not only the dollar smuggling affected Pakistan's economy but also the closure of the border enormous losses to exporters and businessmen. According to media reports, each day border closure is costing local

---

[168] Eltaf Najafizada, Ismail Dilawar, "Dollars Smuggled From Pakistan Provide Lifeline for the Taliban," *Bloomberg*, February 7, 2023
https://www.bloomberg.com/news/articles/2023-02-06/dollars-smuggled-from-pakistan-provide-lifeline-for-the-taliban?leadSource=uverify%20wall

[169] Faheem Jeffery, Interview by Author, March 15, 2023.

traders around Rs100 million.[170] Illegal smuggling is also another factor as it is the major source of income for the population of border settlements. Locals carry goods through illegal routes if the official border is closed, which is their primary source of their income. However, this is not a new trend but after the Taliban takeover, this is trending more.

In the past, Pakistan has spent a lot of money on military operations and it faces a large economic loss, so if the threat of security increases and the state has no other options than to use military means, then yet another burden will be placed on the economy. US officials claim Pakistan received substantial foreign aid and military aid as an outcome of its active role in the 'war on terror' since 9/11. In the past 20 years, the US provided $20 billion in aid to Pakistan, but Pakistani officials are claiming that the country has suffered more than $152 billion in economic losses.[171] It is more difficult for Pakistan this time because the US does not need Islamabad in Afghanistan anymore; their requirements have been fulfilled, and Pakistan's demands are not even taken into account. The sooner the Afghan government build its relations with the international community, the better Pakistan can move forward economically.

3) Refugee Crisis

For more than 40 years, Pakistan has hosted one of the biggest numbers of refugees in the world. In 1978, the

---

[170] Ehtasham Mufti, "Pak-Afghan border closure hits hard 50,000 traders," *The Express Tribune*, October 25, 2021 https://tribune.com.pk/story/2326255/pak-afghan-border-closure-hits-hard-50000-traders

[171] Khurshid Ahmed, "'War on terror' has cost Pakistan more than $150bn in losses since 9/11, officials say," *Arab News*, September 12, 2021 https://www.arabnews.com/node/1927131/world

Saur Revolution led to the first major influx of Afghan refugees into Pakistan. Later on, due to the internal conflict in Afghanistan, Afghan refugees were entering Pakistan consistently. After 9/11, a major migration takes place and a big flow of refugees come to Pakistan. At that time, Pakistan was not expecting that the figure will be increased. According to the United Nations High Commissioner for Refugees (UNHCR), Pakistan is hosting 1.3 million registered Afghan Refugees. According to official estimates, some 600,000 Afghans had also entered Pakistan since August 2021.[172] These are the official figures but in reality, there is a significant number of unregistered Afghan refugees in the country. The re-emergence of the Afghan Taliban has created a humanitarian crisis in Afghanistan.

The Pakistani government has several times announced that it will not grant refugee status to any new Afghan refugees. The government has also stated that it will be cracking down on illegal Afghan immigrants and deporting them back to Afghanistan.[173] However, this decision has been criticized by international human rights organizations, who argue that deporting refugees to Afghanistan, where the security situation is unstable and the Taliban is in power, could put their lives at risk. The Pakistani police recently started a crackdown against illegal Afghan immigrants and send them to

---

[172] "Operational data portal," *UNHCR* https://data.unhcr.org/en/situations/afghanistan

[173] Zofeen T Ebrahim, "Pakistan sends back hundreds of Afghan refugees to face Taliban repression," *The Guardian,* 10 January 2023 https://www.theguardian.com/global-development/2023/jan/10/pakistan-sends-back-hundreds-of-afghan-refugees-to-face-taliban-repression

jail.[174] This crackdown is going on all over the country. The basic reason why people cross the border illegally or didn't have authentic documents like a Passport or a valid visa is that the fee for making a passport is very expensive and also buying a passport from the black market is not working.[175]

After Afghan Taliban came to power in Afghanistan, the flow of refugees increased. The majority of the elite, educated, minority community, as well as the middle class, is leaving Afghanistan for the betterment opportunity and for some people, Pakistan is the easiest way for them.[176] However, the recent influx is putting a strain on the country's resources and infrastructure. There are concerns about security and the potential for extremist elements to infiltrate the refugee population. There have been reports of TTP fighters entering Pakistan disguised as refugees and there are fears that the refugee crisis could exacerbate existing security challenges in the region.

Some individuals and companies are also taking advantage of the vulnerable situation of refugees by offering them jobs with low wages and poor working conditions. This is not only exploitative but also

---

[174] Shah Meer Baloch, "Pakistan crackdown on Afghan refugees leaves 'four dead' and thousands in cells," *The Guardian,* 2 March 2023.
https://www.theguardian.com/global-development/2023/mar/02/pakistan-crackdown-on-afghan-refugees-leaves-four-dead-and-thousands-in-cells

[175] Asma Saayin, "Afghan passports up for grabs in black market," *Pajhwok*, 17 September, 2021
https://pajhwok.com/2021/09/17/afghan-passports-up-for-grabs-in-black-market/

[176] Zofeen T. Ebrahim, "In Pakistan, Afghan refugees face hardship and a frosty reception," *Context news*, April 19, 2022
https://www.context.news/socioeconomic-inclusion/in-pakistan-afghan-refugees-face-hardship-and-a-frosty-reception

contributes to the displacement of local workers, who may be displaced from their jobs as a result. The jobs which were primarily for the residential/native people are given to refugees on a minimum salary.

The situation remains uncertain and it is unclear how the Pakistani government will address the needs of unregistered Afghan refugees in the country. However, it is clear that instability in Afghanistan will continue to drive Afghan refugees to seek safety and protection in neighbouring countries like Pakistan.

4) Border issues

Pakistan-Afghan relations have been strained for decades because of border disputes, ethnic conflicts, and political instability. As a result of the Taliban taking over Afghanistan, border management between the two countries has become even more complicated. There is a long and porous border between them called the Durand Line. Till 2001, the Taliban controlled Afghanistan. Pakistan at that time also raises the Durand line issue with the Taliban but the group refused to negotiate on matters of the Durand line.[177]

After the emergence of the Afghan Taliban, the Taliban's stance on the Durand line has not changed and also the border clashes are increased. Meanwhile, the Taliban Ministry of Defense officials several times condemned Pakistan's fencing of its border with Afghanistan as "illegal."[178]

---

[177] Abhiruchi Chowdhury, "Durand Line and its implication on Pashtuns, " *The Kootneeti*, August 26th, 2020 https://thekootneeti.in/2020/08/26/durand-line-and-its-implication-on-pashtuns/

[178] Kunwar Khuldune Shahid, "Afghanistan and Pakistan's Troubles Won't End With the Taliban Victory," *The Diplomat*, January 26, 2022

Journalist Tahir Khan said that “he didn't think there will be any change in the Afghan policy regarding the Durand line however, the Taliban have a harsher stance as compared to the previous government. During the Ashraf Ghani government, the fencing was never removed but after the Taliban come to power, the fencing has been removed by the group from different places.”[179]

Faheem Jeffery also emphasizes on the similar views that, “the Taliban regime will not shift any policy regarding the Durand line rather their policy will be harder. He said that there will be more problems for Pakistan as we have seen that the border clashes have increased.”[180]

Despite Pakistan's support and sympathies for the Taliban, the group are reiterating the previous stance of the Afghan that Durand Line is an artificial border imposed by the former British Empire.

4.2 OPPORTUNITIES

The re-emergence of the Afghan Taliban in Afghanistan has created opportunities for Pakistan.

1) Trade opportunities and regional connectivity

Pakistan has long been a key player in the region's geopolitics, with a strategic location that connects South Asia with Central Asia, the Middle East, and China. The Taliban's takeover of Afghanistan has raised concerns about security and stability in the region, but it also presents opportunities for Pakistan to enhance its trade and connectivity with Afghanistan and the wider region. In the past, Pakistan has been a major transit route for

---

https://thediplomat.com/2022/01/afghanistan-and-pakistans-troubles-wont-end-with-the-taliban-victory/

[179] Tahir Khan, Interview by Author, March 15, 2023.

[180] Faheem Jeffery, Interview by Author, March 15, 2023.

trade between Afghanistan and other countries and it is well-positioned to benefit from any increase in trade and connectivity. Afghanistan has a large informal economy and much of its trade with Pakistan is conducted through informal channels.[181]

The Taliban's rise to power has raised concerns about the impact on the formal economy, but it also presents an opportunity for Pakistan to engage with the new government and formalize trade relations. There are several areas where Pakistan can potentially benefit from increased trade with Afghanistan. These include agriculture, textiles and construction materials.

According to State Bank of Pakistan (SBP) data, Pakistan's export of goods and services to Afghanistan increased by 10.58 per cent during the current fiscal year (2022-23) as compared to the same period last year (2021-22). During July-January (2022-23), overall exports to Afghanistan reached $285.177 million, an increase of 10.58 per cent over $257.888 million during July-January (2021-22). From $17.384 million in January 2022 to $33.598 million in January 2023, exports to Afghanistan surged by 93.26 percent.[182]

New trade opportunity has built up between both countries in which both can get benefits. Also, Afghanistan-Pakistan Transit Trade Agreement (APTTA) which is a bilateral trade agreement between Pakistan and Afghanistan that was signed in 2010 will also increase the trade opportunity if the situation remains peaceful. The agreement allows Afghan goods

---

[181] "Afghanistan's Informal Economy Size," *World Economics* https://www.worldeconomics.com/National-Statistics/Informal-Economy/Afghanistan.aspx

[182] "Pakistan's exports to Afghanistan increase by 10.8% in seven months," *Daily Times,* March 1, 2023 https://dailytimes.com.pk/1067852/pakistans-exports-to-afghanistan-increase-by-10-8-in-seven-months/

to transit through Pakistan to other countries, and vice versa. The agreement has been instrumental in promoting trade between the two countries, although there have been some issues related to implementation.

Tahir Khan believes that "Pakistan has several opportunities just like in the economic sector Pakistan can increase trade as well as it can connect Islamabad through central Asia. Previously, during the war, several projects were not completed like Turkmenistan–Afghanistan–Pakistan–India (TAPI) Pipeline, the Central Asia-South Asia power project, Rail project but now Pakistan has the opportunity to build up."[183]

Pakistan has long been a proponent of increased regional connectivity, particularly through the China-Pakistan Economic Corridor (CPEC) project. The project aims to connect Pakistan's Gwadar port with China's Xinjiang region through a network of highways, railways, and pipelines. The Taliban's takeover of Afghanistan presents an opportunity to expand this network and connect Afghanistan to the wider region. There are several potential routes for increased connectivity between Pakistan and Afghanistan, including the construction of new highways, railways and pipelines. The development of new ports in Pakistan, such as Gwadar port, could also help to enhance regional connectivity.

Both Pakistan and China are interested in extending the China-Pakistan Economic Corridor (CPEC) to Afghanistan, which will also connect other central Asian countries. [184] There is no doubt that Pakistan has a geopolitical edge over India in Central Asia due to the

---

[183] Tahir Khan, Interview by Author, March 15, 2023.

[184] Kamran Yousaf, "Pakistan, China discuss extending CPEC to Afghanistan," *The Express Tribune*, July 18, 2022 Tribune,https://tribune.com.pk/story/2366540/pakistan-china-discuss-extending-cpec-to-afghanistan

Taliban's presence in Afghanistan. Pakistan's strategic partnership with Central Asian states will be enhanced by a strong, peaceful and stable Afghanistan which will lead to trade opportunities as well as regional connectivity.

2) Refugee support

Taliban's takeover of Kabul has also created hope for the safe return of Afghan refugees in Pakistan, but any return must be voluntary, safe and dignified and the global community must provide the necessary support and assistance to ensure successful reintegration. The decision of Afghan refugees to return to Afghanistan is a very complex subject, influenced by a variety of factors. These include security considerations, economic opportunities, family and social ties and the overall political and social environment in Afghanistan but there are very rare chances but still chances of the return of refugees to their homes.

According to United Nations High Commissioner for Refugees (UNHCR), around 6,029 Afghan refugee voluntarily Repatriation to Afghanistan in 2022 from Pakistan which is a very small number. However, the Taliban's brutal policy towards its people makes it hard for Afghan refugees to return.[185]

3) Peace and Stability

The situation in Afghanistan following the Taliban's return to power in Kabul remains complex but it also gives hope for future stability and peace in Afghanistan. The 20 years old war which was started after the 9/11 attacks ended after the US withdrawal. During this era, not only the Afghan internal situation was worst but also the neighbouring countries were affected by different

---

[185] "Voluntary Repatriation of Afghan Refugees - South West Asia Quarterly Update, 2022 Q4," *UNHCR*, January 25, 2023 https://data.unhcr.org/en/documents/details/98334

means. Almost every state including Pakistan sees Afghanistan through the perspective of security and had played its role in the Afghan conflict to gain there political or other interest but after the conflict end, there is the hope of stability and peace which will also improve the projects of trade and regional connectivity.

While the Taliban have initially announced a general amnesty and protection of minorities, still their promises are not fulfilled and there are already reports of targeted killings, human rights abuses and widespread fear among the population. Although the Taliban's previous regime was marked by harsh and oppressive rule and their return to power has raised concerns among Afghans and the international community about the possibility of a return to such policies. There are also believed that this time Taliban are changed.

However, Faheem, Jeffery didn't agree and believed that, "in his view, there is only one opportunity for those who get benefits from the war. Afghanistan will remain destabilized for the upcoming years. The limited counter-terrorism war will continue either against the Islamic State or any other small groups. Those who were previously getting benefits from the war will get more opportunities. I didn't see any opportunity for Pakistan as a state."[186]

4) Regional Edge:

In light of the Taliban's recent rise to power, Pakistan has a unique comparative advantage over its adversary, India, due to its long-standing close links to the group. As a result of the Taliban's resurgence in Afghanistan, Pakistan now has a direct line of contact with the Taliban leadership and may utilise this connection to advance its strategic objectives in Afghanistan. This gives Pakistan a substantial competitive edge in the region.

---

[186] Faheem Jeffery, Interview by Author, March 15, 2023.

According to Pakistan, the previous administration assisted and permitted India to establish a strategic position against Pakistan. India, with the assistance of the Kabul administration, utilised Afghan land against Islamabad by supporting Baloch terrorists and the TTP.[187] With the overthrow of an Afghan government, the chance to stop India's structural presence and its exploitation of Afghan territory against Pakistan emerged.

India's development initiatives and diplomatic mission in Afghanistan had to be suspended due to the Taliban's takeover. It is also significant that New Delhi was among the few nations to oppose the Taliban's process of reconciliation. India has long been an ally of anti-Taliban troops and has voiced its opposition to the Taliban in various international fora, including the UN.[188] Further evidence of Pakistan's influence in Afghanistan can be found in the fact that the group sought the advice of General Qamar Javed Bajwa, the then-army chief, before asking India to send its diplomats and technical staff to Kabul.[189]

Given that the Taliban are once again in power, Pakistan's backing for the organisation may prevent India from participating in any future discussions and

---

[187] Ayaz Gul, "Pakistan Claims 'Irrefutable Evidence' of Indian Links to Terrorism on Pakistani Soil," *Voice of America*, November 14, 2020 https://www.voanews.com/a/south-central-asia_pakistan-claims-irrefutable-evidence-indian-links-terrorism-pakistani-soil/6198372.html

[188] Kamran Yousaf, "Why is India embracing the Afghan Taliban?" *The Express Tribune*, June 06, 2022 https://tribune.com.pk/story/2360222/why-is-india-embracing-the-afghan-taliban

[189] Anwar Iqbal, "Taliban consulted Gen Bajwa before reaching out to India," *Dawn*, April 26, 2023 https://www.dawn.com/news/1749344

negotiations regarding the future of Afghanistan, giving Pakistan an advantage in their geopolitical rivalry.

The Taliban's control of Afghanistan has also provided Pakistan with a regional as well as geopolitical advantage over India in the wider Central Asian region. A stable Afghanistan might help Pakistan accomplish its geoeconomic goals in the region by acting as a strategic link between Islamabad and the Central Asian countries.

5) Counterterrorism cooperation:

Pakistan and Afghanistan have an opportunity to do Counterterrorism cooperation against Islamic State (IS) in the region. Although, doing counter-terrorism cooperation between Pakistan and the Afghan Taliban is extremely difficult because of Tehreek-e-Taliban Pakistan's (TTP) factor but both are facing significant security challenges posed by the presence of the Islamic State (IS) so there are quite chances for cooperation.

The rise of IS in Afghanistan has added a new layer of complexity to the country's already complex security environment and the group has launched several attacks against both Afghan and Pakistani security forces and civilians. The Islamic State has claimed around 400 attacks in Afghanistan and Pakistan's Khyber Pakhtunkhwa area since Kabul's fall. IS also targets the minority Shia community, which is fueling sectarian unrest.[190]

"Pakistan is also facing a big threat from the Islamic State not only inside Pakistan but also in Afghanistan as Pakistan's interests are sabotaged." Faheem Jeffery

---

[190] Colin P. Clarke, "Islamic State Khorasan Province Is a Growing Threat in Afghanistan and Beyond," *The Diplomat,* April 29, 2023. https://thediplomat.com/2023/04/islamic-state-khorasan-province-is-a-growing-threat-in-afghanistan-and-beyond/

said.[191]

There is undoubtedly a chance in this situation for Pakistan and Afghanistan to collaborate on counterterrorism activities. To prevent the passage of extremists across the border, such collaboration required the sharing of intelligence, conducting coordinated actions, and upgrading border security measures.

About Taliban's current position, Tahir Khan said that, "Taliban will remain in power and there is no immediate threat to them. They have built their Army, Police and also, they put their officials in different institutions so that they can control the ruling structure. They are strengthening their system," adding that "currently, there is no alternative to the Taliban. The other opposition parties are so weak. The world is giving time to the Taliban so that Taliban can review their policies however yet there are no such actions scenes from them," Tahir Khan said.[192]

"Far away there is no chance that the Taliban government end or finish. There is only one possibility if there is an internal rift inside the Taliban which led towards an armed struggle and weak the Taliban government but currently, this will never happen," Faheem Jeffery also shares the similar views adding that, "whenever Western countries will get a chance, they will double-cross the Afghan Taliban with different means but currently, there are no such states who are going to support any armed resistance against the Taliban.[193]

Jeffery further emphasises that "the regional countries' roles have increased because in future if there is any

---

[191] Faheem Jeffery, Interview by Author, March 15, 2023.
[192] Tahir Khan, Interview by Author, March 15, 2023.
[193] Faheem Jeffery, Interview by Author, March 15, 2023.

issue or instability in Afghanistan then the regional countries will play their role rather US, NATO or Western countries because the US already wasted 20 years and they are not willing to come again."[194]

In conclusion, Pakistan has faced both obstacles and opportunities as a result of the Afghan Taliban's resurgence. By facilitating negotiations between the international community, offering aid, encouraging economic cooperation, addressing global issues, enhancing border security and promoting inter-group contacts, Islamabad can significantly contribute to the stability and peace in Afghanistan. By taking a positive and proactive stance, Pakistan can contribute to ensuring that Afghanistan has a stable and successful future, which will benefit the entire region.

---

[194] Ibid

CONCLUSION

Pakistan-Afghanistan has deep-rooted relations linked with culture, language as well as religious factors. These historical and societal ties have played a major part in shaping the two countries' bilateral relationship. States and their fortunes are inextricably linked and the states become mutually dependent and vulnerable to one another's actions.

It is also a fact that the state's behaviour directly impacts its neighbouring states. In the case of Pak-Afghan, this is exactly correct and one state domestic factors are directly affecting others. Historically, Kabul and Islamabad relations have conflicting tie as both sees and formulate policy on the military angle. While economic sector was neglected. Both also cooperated in various sectors and have occasional tensions.

As it is the reality that you can change friends, not neighbours, and also the past cannot change, but the future can be better. Despite being an ally of the US in the war against terrorism, Pakistan was accused of providing support to the Taliban, although Pakistan officially denies the allegations but reality can't be ignored. As now the Taliban are in power and consider a close ally of Islamabad, there are more challenges as compare to opportunities for Pakistan.

The Taliban's re-acquisition of power prompts worries about regional stability, potential violence escalation and the escalation of already-present security problems within Pakistan. Numerous difficulties are presented by the refugee crisis and its effects on Pakistan's already frail economy. Security concerns, economic repercussions, a potential refugee catastrophe and increased drug trafficking dangers are among the major effects of the Afghan Taliban in power. To address these concerns, Pakistan would need to take a proactive and comprehensive strategy.

The presence of the Taliban in Afghanistan may also encourage extremist elements within Pakistan, calling for increased security precautions and strict border controls. The internal stability of Pakistan is also threatened by it.

Despite these difficulties, Pakistan has a chance to contribute in a positive way to promote stability and peace in by assisting the Afghan peace process, strive towards a thorough political engagement and help establish a climate favourable to lasting peace by making use of its position as a regional power. As members of South Asia and Central Asia, Islamabad and Kabul can be crucial players in initiatives aimed at regional integration, such as the creation of trade routes and connectivity initiatives.

Also, Pakistan has a unique opportunity to take advantage of Afghanistan's strategic locations for its economic interest. Kabul can act as a hub for transit trade and business because of its borders with China, Iran and particularly Central Asian nations. Pakistan recently also starts taking advantage of Afghanistan's land as the shipment of liquefied petroleum gas (LPGP) from Turkmenistan, which was transported through the southern Afghan province of Kandahar reached Pakistan.[195] Islamabad in partnership with Central Asian countries is also seeking to establish liquefied natural gas (LNG) plants in Gwadar, which will attract

---

[195] "Turkmenistan LPG starts reaching Pakistan via Afghanistan," *The News*, May 01, 2023 https://www.thenews.com.pk/print/1065862-turkmenistan-lpg-starts-reaching-pakistan-via-afghanistan

investments from various countries.[196]

Similarly, Pakistan is also looking towards the new international Central Asian markets as this region has diverse natural resources which will also fill Pakistan's requirements. It is also a fact that Pakistan's ambition can only be fulfilled if Afghanistan has a government who are more inclined towards Islamabad and with the past experiment it seems that the Taliban is more acceptable for Pakistan.

Islamabad may gain economically from the Taliban's resurgence. Trade routes and commercial opportunities would be made available if Kabul was more stable. In order to connect Central Asian countries that are landlocked with seaports and markets, Pakistan can position itself as a significant commerce and transit centre. In addition to helping Pakistan's economy, this improved regional connection would promote regional development and integration. Pakistan's involvement in Afghanistan's rehabilitation would improve bilateral relations and promote economic cooperation.

However, there are mostly positive, inspirational and fictional stories regarding the re-emergence of the Afghan Taliban in Pakistan but in reality, Islamabad is going to suffer more. The security conditions and the response from the Afghan authorities seem that Kabul is not serious to consider Pakistan's serious concerns regarding the security matter. Although, Pakistan and Afghanistan are doing economic collaboration but its ratio is not enough as the region has vast potential for economic activities and trade. Economic activities in the region are also disrupted since China wants to expand the Belt and Road Initiative (BRI) and China-Pakistan

---

[196] Israr Khan, "Pakistan seeks energy partnership with Central Asia," *The News*, June 22, 2023 https://www.thenews.com.pk/print/1083118-pakistan-seeks-energy-partnership-with-central-asia

Economic Corridor (CPEC) into Afghanistan but is concerned about security.

It also seems that in future whenever the Taliban wants to hold a discussion with the Pakistani authority, they will mostly discuss trade as well as economic opportunity but on the Pakistani side, they have nothing to talk except security concerns.

Islamabad needs to take a comprehensive approach if it wants to take advantage of chances. To maximise the economic potential, it should put diplomatic engagement first, take advantage of regional alliances, and invest in infrastructural development. Pakistan must also keep up its fight against extremist beliefs and strengthen internal security measures at the same time to ensure that the Taliban's resurgence does not jeopardise the country's stability.

While economic cooperation is only possible when there is peace and stability. When the region or a state is insecure there is no chance of any foreign investment or cooperation. While in the Pak-Afghan case, the economic concerns seem to be addressed while the major security challenge that Pakistan has on several occasions raised does not seem to be solved soon. Afghan Taliban will use Tehreek-e-Taliban-e-Pakistan (TTP) as a proxy against Pakistan. The other militant groups such as Islamic State (IS) will also take the advantage of the scenario and increase their activities. While Islamabad has the capability to deal with the militant group as previously, they have already conducted major military operations but later on, the militant groups re-emerged because Afghanistan was providing safe heavens to them. Due to this situation, Pakistan will suffer but the tribal region will suffer more as it will be the main ground for war. Now the situation on the ground is more favourable to the militant groups as the Afghan side will not use any force against them.

BIBLIOGRAPHY

Munir, Asad, "The Faqir of Ipi of North Waziristan," The Express Tribune, 2010

https://tribune.com.pk/story/77388/the-faqir-of-ipi-of-north-waziristan

Afghan Peace Accord (Islamabad Accord)," Peace agreement database

Arnold, Anthony, "Afghanistan Two Party Communism: Parcham and Khalaq," California: Hoover Institution Press, 1985, p 45.

"Afghanistan: Crisis of Impunity," Human Rights Watch, July 2001, Vol. 13, No. 3, p.15.

"Al-Qaeda and Osama bin Laden," Daily Outlook Afghanistan,

July 06, 2020

http://outlookafghanistan.net/topics.php?post_id=26928

"Afghan Study Group Final Report: A Pathway for Peace in Afghanistan," US Institute of Peace, February 3, 2021

Ali, Obaid and Clark, Kate, "A Quarter of Afghanistan's Districts Fall to the Taleban amid Calls for a 'Second Resistance,'" Afghanistan Analysts Network, July 2, 2021.

"Afghanistan crisis: Taliban kill civilians in resistance stronghold," BBC, September 13, 2021.

"Al Qaeda Could Rebuilt in Afghanistan in a Year or Two, US Officials Say," New York Times, September 14, 2021.

Ali, Manzoor, "KP police chief calls IS-K bigger threat than TTP," DAWN, January 21, 2022

https://www.dawn.com/news/1670641

"Afghan militia leaders Atta Noor, Dostum escape 'conspiracy'," Reuters, August 15, 2021

https://www.reuters.com/world/asia-pacific/afghan-militia-leaders-atta-noor-dostum-escape-conspiracy-2021-08-14/

Ahmed, Khurshid, "'War on terror' has cost Pakistan more than $150bn in losses since 9/11, officials say," Arab News,

September 12, 2021

https://www.arabnews.com/node/1927131/world

"Afghanistan's Informal Economy Size," World Economics

https://www.worldeconomics.com/National-Statistics/Informal-Economy/Afghanistan.aspx

"Annual Threat Assessment of the U.S. Intelligence Community, Office of the Director of National Intelligence," April 09, 2021

https://www.dni.gov/files/ODNI/documents/assessments/ATA-2021-Unclassified-Report.pdf

Balouch, Akhtar "The mystery that shrouds Liaquat Ali Khan's murder," Dawn, 2015

https://www.dawn.com/news/1213461

Brasseur, Brad L, "Recognising the Durand Line: A Way Forward for Afghanistan and Pakistan?," The East West Institute, 2011

Biswas, Arka, " Durand Line: History, Legality & Future," Occasional Paper, 2013

Bazai, Abdul Manan, "An assessment of Pak-Afghan relations, Since 1947 up to 2001," p. 27

http://prr.hec.gov.pk/jspui/bitstream/123456789/877/1/1899S.pdf

Bazai, Abdul Manan, "An assessment of Pak-Afghan relations, Since 1947 up to 2001," p. 27

http://prr.hec.gov.pk/jspui/bitstream/123456789/877/1/1899S.pdf

Bazai, Abdul Manan, "An assessment of Pak-Afghan relations, Since 1947 up to 2001," p. 79

http://prr.hec.gov.pk/jspui/bitstream/123456789/877/1/1899S.pdf

Bazai, Abdul Manan, "An assessment of Pak-Afghan relations, Since 1947 up to 2001," p. 109

http://prr.hec.gov.pk/jspui/bitstream/123456789/877/1/1899S

.pdf

Bazai, Abdul Manan, "An assessment of Pak-Afghan relations, Since 1947 up to 2001," p. 25

http://prr.hec.gov.pk/jspui/bitstream/123456789/877/1/1899S.pdf

Bazai, Abdul Manan, "An assessment of Pak-Afghan relations, Since 1947 up to 2001," p. 1

http://prr.hec.gov.pk/jspui/bitstream/123456789/877/1/1899S.pdf

Bazai, Abdul Manan, "An assessment of Pak-Afghan relations, Since 1947 up to 2001," p. 69

http://prr.hec.gov.pk/jspui/bitstream/123456789/877/1/1899S.pdf

Bazai, Abdul Manan, "An assessment of Pak-Afghan relations, Since 1947 up to 2001," p. 148

http://prr.hec.gov.pk/jspui/bitstream/123456789/877/1/1899S.pdf

Bazai, Abdul Manan, "An assessment of Pak-Afghan relations, Since 1947 up to 2001," p. 149

http://prr.hec.gov.pk/jspui/bitstream/123456789/877/1/1899S.pdf

Bazai, Abdul Manan, "An assessment of Pak-Afghan relations, Since 1947 up to 2001," p. 168

http://prr.hec.gov.pk/jspui/bitstream/123456789/877/1/1899S.pdf

Bazai, Abdul Manan, "An assessment of Pak-Afghan relations, Since 1947 up to 2001," p. 175

http://prr.hec.gov.pk/jspui/bitstream/123456789/877/1/1899S.pdf

Bazai, Abdul Manan, "An assessment of Pak-Afghan relations, Since 1947 up to 2001," p. 177

http://prr.hec.gov.pk/jspui/bitstream/123456789/877/1/1899S.pdf

Bijlert, Martine van, "The Focus of the Taleban's New Government: Internal cohesion, external dominance," Afghanistan Analysts Network, September 12, 2021.

Baloch, Shah Meer, "Pakistan crackdown on Afghan refugees leaves 'four dead' and thousands in cells," The Guardian, 2 March 2023.

https://www.theguardian.com/global-development/2023/mar/02/pakistan-crackdown-on-afghan-refugees-leaves-four-dead-and-thousands-in-cells

Condon, Bernard and Watson, Julie, "Rescue groups: US tally misses hundreds left in Afghanistan," Associated Press, September 4, 2021.

"Concerns over US terror threat rising as Taliban hold grows," Associated Press, August 15, 2021.

https://apnews.com/article/joe-biden-taliban-ffa2ce2739f5be13e73db65c4a93cd54

Chowdhury, Abhiruchi, "Durand Line and its implication on Pashtuns, " The Kootneeti, August 26th, 2020

https://thekootneeti.in/2020/08/26/durand-line-and-its-implication-on-pashtuns/

Caltrider, Mac, "UPDATE: 'LION OF HERAT' REPORTEDLY IN IRAN FOLLOWING TALIBAN CAPTURE," Coffee or Die, August 19, 2021

https://coffeeordie.com/ismail-khan-herat-iran

Clarke, Colin P, "Islamic State Khorasan Province Is a Growing Threat in Afghanistan and Beyond," The Diplomat, April 29, 2023.

https://thediplomat.com/2023/04/islamic-state-khorasan-province-is-a-growing-threat-in-afghanistan-and-beyond/

Dxit, J.N and Hussan, Dr Riffat, "The Anatomy of a Conflict: Afghanistan and 9/11," Paul Press, Okhla, New Delhi, 2002 p.198-199

Donovan, Jeffrey, "Afghanistan: Bush Likens U.S. Effort To Marshall Plan," Radio Free Europe/Radio Liberty, April 2002 https://www.rferl.org/a/1099500.html

"Donald Trump isolationist doctrine "America first": A case study of the US withdrawal from Afghanistan," University Mohamed Boudiaf

Dilawar, Ismail and Najafizada, Eltaf, "Dollars Smuggled From Pakistan Provide Lifeline for the Taliban," Bloomberg, February 7, 2023

https://www.bloomberg.com/news/articles/2023-02-06/dollars-smuggled-from-pakistan-provide-lifeline-for-the-taliban?leadSource=uverify%20wall

Ebrahim , Zofeen T, "Pakistan sends back hundreds of Afghan refugees to face Taliban repression," The Guardian, 10 January 2023

https://www.theguardian.com/global-development/2023/jan/10/pakistan-sends-back-hundreds-of-afghan-refugees-to-face-taliban-repression

Ebrahim , Zofeen T, "In Pakistan, Afghan refugees face hardship and a frosty reception," Context news, April 19, 2022

https://www.context.news/socioeconomic-inclusion/in-pakistan-afghan-refugees-face-hardship-and-a-frosty-reception

"Ex-president hanged by Taliban after fall of Kabul," Irish Time, Sep 28 1996

https://www.irishtimes.com/news/ex-president-hanged-by-taliban-after-fall-of-kabul-1.90501

"FACTBOX: Five Facts on Taliban Leader Mullah Mohammad Omar," Reuters, November 17, 2008

https://www.reuters.com/article/us-afghan-taliban-omar-idUSTRE4AG1EM20081117

Gul, Imtiaz, "The Unholy Nexus: Pak-Afghan relations Under the Taliban," Vanguard, 2002, 11-12

Ghubar, Gulabudin, "Taliban Blames Govt for Delay in Peace Talks," Tolo News, July 19, 2020

https://tolonews.com/afghanistan/taliban-blames-govt-delay-peace-talks

Grare, Frédéric, "Pakistan-Afghanistan relations in the post-9/11 era," Carnegie Papers, 2006, p. 17

https://carnegieendowment.org/files/cp72_grare_final.pdf

Gall, Carlotta, "Taliban Surges as U.S. Shifts Some Tasks to NATO," New York Times, June 11, 2006.

Goodson, Larry P. Larry, "Afghanistan's Endless War: State Failure, Regional Politics, and the Rise of the Taliban," University of Washington Press, 2001

Gul, Ayaz, "Pakistan Claims 'Irrefutable Evidence' of Indian Links to Terrorism on Pakistani Soil," Voice of America, November 14, 2020

https://www.voanews.com/a/south-central-asia_pakistan-claims-irrefutable-evidence-indian-links-terrorism-pakistani-soil/6198372.html

Hali, Sultan M, "Breaking the myths of Pakistan ruining Afghanistan," Pakistan Today

https://archive.pakistantoday.com.pk/2016/08/12/breaking-the-myths-of-pakistan-ruining-afghanistan/

Hunarmal, Mohammad Hussain, "The formidable Faqir," The News, 2021

https://www.thenews.com.pk/tns/detail/789500-the-formidable-faqir

Hudson, John, "Trump directed aides to reduce U.S. troops in Afghanistan by 2020 election, Pompeo says," The Washington Post, July 29, 2019

https://www.washingtonpost.com/world/national-security/trump-directed-aides-to-reduce-us-troops-in-afghanistan-by-2020-election-pompeo-says/2019/07/29/5546df7d-d2fd-443f-ae05-e78bab070bad_story.html

Haqqani, Hussain, "Pakistan: Between the Mosque and the Military," op. cit,170.

Haqqani, Hussain, "Pakistan: Between the Mosque and the

Military," Carnegie Endowment for International Peace, 2005. op. cit, 170.

Hali, Sultan M, "Breaking the myths of Pakistan ruining Afghanistan," Pakistan Today

https://archive.pakistantoday.com.pk/2016/08/12/breaking-the-myths-of-pakistan-ruining-afghanistan/

Hali, Sultan M, "Breaking the myths of Pakistan ruining Afghanistan," Pakistan Today

https://archive.pakistantoday.com.pk/2016/08/12/breaking-the-myths-of-pakistan-ruining-afghanistan/

Hali, Sultan M, "Breaking the myths of Pakistan ruining Afghanistan," Pakistan Today

https://archive.pakistantoday.com.pk/2016/08/12/breaking-the-myths-of-pakistan-ruining-afghanistan/

Hussain, Rifaat "PAKISTAN'S RELATIONS WITH AFGHANISTAN: CONTINUITY AND CHANGE," Institute of Strategic Studies Islamabad, 2002

Hussain, Zahid, "Frontline Pakistan the Struggle with Militant Islam," Vanguard Books, 2007

House, White, "Remarks by President Biden on the Way Forward in Afghanistan," April 14, 2021.

Hussain, Abid, "What is behind a resurgence of violent attacks in Pakistan?," Al Jazeera, 26 Dec 2022

https://www.aljazeera.com/news/2022/12/26/what-is-behind-a-resurgence-of-violent-attacks-in-pakistan

Hussain, Abid, "Pakistan Taliban threatens top political leadership including PM," Al Jazeera, 4 January, 2023

https://www.aljazeera.com/news/2023/1/4/pakistan-taliban-threatens-top-political-leadership-including-pm

"In February 1958, Mohammad Zahir Shah, the king of Afghanistan, visited India after an official visit to Pakistan," Global Indian.

https://www.globalindian.com/galleryandvideos/global-indian-museum/mohammad-zahir-shah-visited-india-1958/

Iqbal, Anwar, "Taliban consulted Gen Bajwa before reaching out to India," Dawn, April 26, 2023

https://www.dawn.com/news/1749344

Ibid

Jeffery, Faheem, Interview by Author, March 15, 2023.

Kux, Dennis, "The United States and Pakistan, 1947-2000: Disenchanted Allies," Woodrow Wilson, 2001, p. 252

Kux, Dennis, "The United States and Pakistan, 1947-2000: Disenchanted Allies," Woodrow Wilson, 2001, op. cit, p. 274

Kux, Dennis, "The United States and Pakistan, 1947-2000: Disenchanted Allies," Woodrow Wilson, 2001, op. cit, p. 247

Kronstadt, K. Alan, "Terrorism in South Asia," CRS Report for Congress, 2004.

Kakar, Rafiullah, "Pak-Afghan Relations: Tracing the Roots of Troubled Past (1947-2001)," Journal of Asian Politics & History, 2012

Khan, Iftikhar A, "Terror attacks in Pakistan surge by 51pc after Afghan Taliban victory," DAWN, October 20, 2022

https://www.dawn.com/news/1715927

Khan, Tahir, Interview by Author, March 15, 2023.

Khan, Israr, "Pakistan seeks energy partnership with Central Asia," The News, June 22, 2023

https://www.thenews.com.pk/pri

Lamb, Robert D and Tarzi, Amin, "Measuring Perceptions About the Pashtun People," Center for Strategic and International Studies, 2011

https://csis-website-prod.s3.amazonaws.com/s3fs-public/legacy_files/files/publication/110316_Lamb_PashtunPerceptions_web.pdf

Mufti, Ehtasham, "Pak-Afghan border closure hits hard 50,000 traders," The Express Tribune, October 25, 2021

https://tribune.com.pk/story/2326255/pak-afghan-border-closure-hits-hard-50000-traders

Musharraf, Pervez, "In the Line of fire," Simon & Schuster, 2006

"Mullah Baradar released by Pakistan at the behest of US: Khalilzad," The Hindu, February 9, 2019

Mazari, Shireen, "The Durand Line: Evolution of an International Frontier," Strategic Studies vol. 2, no. 2 (Autumn 1978): 45

Mir, Hamid, "Afghanistan's pipeline police", September 17, 2002. http://www.rediff.com/news/2002/sep/17guest.htm (accessed on January 18, 2012)

Miller et al., Zeke, "Biden team surprised by rapid Taliban gains in Afghanistan," Associated Press, August 15, 2021.

"Mohammad Zahir Shah (1933–73)," Britannica

https://www.britannica.com/place/Afghanistan/Mohammad-Zahir-Shah-1933-73

Maley, William, "Afghanistan and the Taliban: The Rebirth of Fundamentalism?, New York University Press, 1998, p. 43-47

Nasar, Khudai Noor, "Afghanistan: Taliban leaders in bust-up at presidential palace, sources say," BBC, September 15, 2021.

"Najeebullah announces to tender resignation," Afghan Islamic Press, 19 March, 1992

https://www.afghanislamicpress.com/en/news/32063

Nye, Joseph S and Keohane, Robert O, "Power and Interdependence Revisited, International Organization," The MIT Press, 1977

"Operational data portal," UNHCR

https://data.unhcr.org/en/situations/afghanistan

Olaf Caroe, Olaf, "The Pathans." Oxford University Press, 1958

"Pashtunistan - 1947-1955," Global Security

https://www.globalsecurity.org/military/world/war/pashtunistan-1947.htm

"Pakistan's Role in Global War on Terrorism: and Areas of Clash with United States," Pakistan Defence,

http://www.defence.pk/forums/strategic-geopoliticalissues/29111-pakistan-s-role-global-war-terrorism-areas-clash-united-states.html (accessed Januray 20, 2022)

"Pakistan: Countering Global Terrorism," Institute of Regional Studies, Islamabad, 16.

"Pakistan says decision to boycott Bonn conference is final," The Express Tribune, 2011

https://tribune.com.pk/story/300020/pakistan-says-decision-to-boycott-bonn-conference-is-final

"Peshawar Accord," Peace agreement database

"Pashtunistan - 1947-1955," Global Security

https://www.globalsecurity.org/military/world/war/pashtunistan-1947.htm#google_vignette

"Pakistan's exports to Afghanistan increase by 10.8% in seven months," Daily Times, March 1, 2023

https://dailytimes.com.pk/1067852/pakistans-exports-to-afghanistan-increase-by-10-8-in-seven-months/

Rahi, Arwin, "Afghanistan and Pakistan's oft-ignored history – 1947-1978," The Express Tribune, September, 10, 2020

https://tribune.com.pk/article/97165/afghanistan-and-pakistans-oft-ignored-history-1947-1978

"Res transit cum suo onere" Oxford Reference

https://www.oxfordreference.com/display/10.1093/acref/9780195369380.001.0001/acref-9780195369380-e-1847;jsessionid=3EDA2061E43A65A6EBD7C98E15BA2427#:~:text=%E2%80%9CA%20thing%20passes%20away%20with,the%20territory%20or%20property%20itself.

Rashid, Ahmed, "Taliban: Islam, Oil, and the New Great Game in Central Asia, Tauris, 2002, p.18

Rahi, Arwin, "The Durand Line: Separating myth from reality," The Express Tribune, 2022 https://tribune.com.pk/article/97542/the-durand-line-separating-myth-from-reality

Roy, Oliver, "Islam and Resistance in Afghanistan," Cambridge University Press,

Rasanayagam, Angelo, "Afghanistan: A Modern History," I.B. Tauris, p. 103

Rashid, Ahmed "Taliban: Militant Islam, Oil and Fundamentalism in Central Asia Paperback," Yale University Press, 2010

Rashid, Ahmed, Jihad the Rise of Militant Islam in Central Asia, op.cit., 184.

"Rumsfeld: Major combat over in Afghanistan," CNN, May 1, 2003.

Rubin, Barnett, "Turmoil in the Taliban," New Yorker, July 31, 2015

"Remarks by President Biden on the Way Forward in Afghanistan," The White House, April 14, 2021

https://www.whitehouse.gov/briefing-room/speeches-remarks/2021/04/14/remarks-by-president-biden-on-the-way-forward-in-afghanistan/

"Remarks by President Biden on the Way Forward in Afghanistan," The White House, April 14, 2021

https://www.whitehouse.gov/briefing-room/speeches-remarks/2021/04/14/remarks-by-president-biden-on-the-way-forward-in-afghanistan/

"Remarks by President Biden on the End of the War in Afghanistan,"

https://www.whitehouse.gov/briefing-room/speeches-remarks/2021/08/31/remarks-by-president-biden-on-the-end-of-the-war-in-afghanistan/

"Russia says US plan for troop pullout from Afghanistan risks 'escalation," Al Arabiya News,

https://english.alarabiya.net/News/world/2021/04/14/Russia-says-US-plan-for-troop-pullout-from-Afghanistan-risks-escalation-

Robertson, Nic, “Taliban removes security from ex-Afghan President Hamid Karzai and Abdullah Abdullah, source says,” CNN, August 26, 2021.

Rowlatt, Justin, “Taliban open letter to Trump urges Afghan withdrawal,” BBC, August 15, 2017

Rahman, Hanif-ur, "Pak-Afghan Relations during Z.A. Bhutto Era: The Dynamics of Cold War," Pakistan Journal of History and Culture, Vol. XXXIII, No.2, 2012, p 9

http://www.nihcr.edu.pk/Latest_English_Journal/Jrnl%2033-2%20(2012)%20PDF/2.%20Pak-Afghan%20Relations,%20hanif%20khan.pdf

Rahman, Hanif-ur, "Pak-Afghan Relations during Z.A. Bhutto Era: The Dynamics of Cold War," Pakistan Journal of History and Culture, Vol. XXXIII, No.2, 2012, p 10

http://www.nihcr.edu.pk/Latest_English_Journal/Jrnl%2033-2%20(2012)%20PDF/2.%20Pak-Afghan%20Relations,%20hanif%20khan.pdf

Safdar, Malik and Ali, Dr Muhammad, "Pakistan Afghan Relation History Conflicts and challenges," Pak. Journal of Int'L Affairs, Vol 3, Issue 2 (2020)

"Splintering relations?: Durand Line is a 'settled issue', says FO," The Express Tribune, 2012

https://tribune.com.pk/story/456881/splintering-relations-durand-line-is-a-settled-issue-says-fo/

Shah, Dr Baber, "Geo-Strategic Patterns of a post-Taliban Afghanistan, Strategic Studies, Islamabad, 2002, p.45

Safdar, Malik and Ali, Dr Muhammad, "Pakistan Afghan Relation History Conflicts and challenges," Pak. Journal of Int'L Affairs, Vol 3, Issue 2 (2020), p. 405

Shah, Sabir, "NAP was banned twice by Yahya and Bhutto," The News, 2015

https://www.thenews.com.pk/print/38435-nap-was-banned-twice-by-yahya-and-bhutto

Sattar, Abdul, “Afghanistan: Past, Present and Future, From Jihad to Civil War”, The Institute of Regional Studies, Islamabad, 1997, pp. 462-63

"Suspected U.S. Missile Strike Kills 18 in Pakistan", Associated Press, January 23, 2009.

Musharraf, Pervez, "In the Line of fire," Simon & Schuster, 2006, p. 201

"Secret Joint Raid Captures Taliban’s Top Commander," The New York Times, 2010

https://www.nytimes.com/2010/02/16/world/asia/16intel.html

Shah, Taimoor and Mashal, Mujib, “Taliban’s New Leader, More Scholar Than Fighter, Is Slow to Impose Himself,” The New York Times, 2016

https://www.nytimes.com/2016/07/12/world/asia/taliban-afghanistan-pakistan-mawlawi-haibatullah-akhundzada.html

Schmitt, Eric and Mashal, Mujib, “White House Orders Direct Taliban Talks to Jump-Start Afghan Negotiations,” The New York Times, 2018

https://www.nytimes.com/2018/07/15/world/asia/afghanistan-taliban-direct-negotiations.html

“Senate Armed Services Committee Holds Hearing on the Defense Budget Posture,” CQ, March 4, 2020.

“Statement of Islamic Emirate regarding recent announcement by US President Joe Biden,” Voice of Jihad, April 15, 2021.

“Some Afghans Blame Neighboring Pakistan for Taliban Gains,” Associated Press, August 12, 2021

Schroden, Jonathan, “Afghanistan Security Forces Versus the Taliban: A Net Assessment,” CTC Sentinel, Vol. 14, Issue 1, January 2021.

Smith, Saphora, Yusufzai, Mushtaq and Luce, Dan De, “Even the Taliban are surprised at how fast they’re advancing in Afghanistan,” NBC News, June 25, 2021.

Saayin, Asma, "Afghan passports up for grabs in black

market," Pajhwok, 17 September, 2021

https://pajhwok.com/2021/09/17/afghan-passports-up-for-grabs-in-black-market/

Shahid, Kunwar Khuldune, "Afghanistan and Pakistan's Troubles Won't End With the Taliban Victory," The Diplomat, January 26, 2022

https://thediplomat.com/2022/01/afghanistan-and-pakistans-troubles-wont-end-with-the-taliban-victory/

"Taliban announce creation of Islamic Emirate of Afghanistan, will rule country through council," DAWN, August 19, 2021

https://www.dawn.com/news/1641540

"Terror attacks in Pakistan surge by 51pc after Afghan Taliban victory." DAWN, October 20, 2022

https://www.dawn.com/news/1715927

"Taliban and Mullah Omar," Daily Lead Pakistan, July 12, 2020

https://leadpakistan.com.pk/news/taliban-and-mullah-omar/

Tanne, Stephen "Afghanistan: A Military History from Alexander the Great to the War against the Taliban," Da Capo Press, 2009, p. 276

"Taliban and Mullah Omar," Daily Lead Pakistan, July 12, 2020

https://leadpakistan.com.pk/news/taliban-and-mullah-omar/

The White House, "Remarks by President Biden on the End of the War in Afghanistan," August 31, 2021.

"Text: President Bush Addresses the Nation," The Washington Post, Sept, 20, 2001

https://www.washingtonpost.com/wp-srv/nation/specials/attacked/transcripts/bushaddress_092001.html

Tenet, George, "At the Center of the Storm: My Years at the CIA, (New York," Harper Collins, 2007, 182-183

"Taliban not living up to its commitments, U.S. Defense

Secretary says," Reuters, May 5, 2020.

"The Durand Line, A historic, disputed border separates Afghanistan and Pakistan," National Geography

https://education.nationalgeographic.org/resource/durand-line/

"The situation in Afghanistan," United Nations, 2020

http://unscr.com/en/resolutions/doc/2513

"The situation in Afghanistan," United Nations, 1999

http://unscr.com/en/resolutions/doc/1267

"Turkmenistan LPG starts reaching Pakistan via Afghanistan," The News, May 01, 2023

https://www.thenews.com.pk/print/1065862-turkmenistan-lpg-starts-reaching-pakistan-via-afghanistan

"UAE Ministry of Foreign Affairs and International Cooperation, Statement on President Ashraf Ghani," August 18 2021.

"United Nations Arms Embargoes, Their Impact on Arms Flows and Target Behaviour," Stockholm International Peace Research Institute, 2007, p 06

https://www.sipri.org/sites/default/files/files/misc/UNAE/SIPRI07UNAETal.pdf

"U.S. Is Quietly Reducing Its Troop Force in Afghanistan," New York Times, October 21, 2019.

US Department of Defense, "Secretary of Defense Austin and Chairman of the Joint Chiefs of Staff Gen. Milley Press Briefing," September 1, 2021.

Usman, Tehseena, "Trust Deficit in Pak-Afghan Relations and its

Implications: A Historical Perspective (1947-2001)"

Usman, Tehseena, "Trust Deficit in Pak-Afghan Relations and its Implications: A Historical Perspective (1947-2001)," p 9

https://www.qurtuba.edu.pk/thedialogue/The%20Dialogue/8_3/Dialogue_July_September2013_303-326.pdf

"Vienna Convention on Succession of States in respect of Treaties," UN, 1978

https://legal.un.org/ilc/texts/instruments/english/conventions/3_2_1978.pdf

“Violence ‘Not Consistent’ with US-Taliban Deal: US Envoy,” TOLOnews, October 13, 2020.

"Voluntary Repatriation of Afghan Refugees - South West Asia Quarterly Update, 2022 Q4," UNHCR, January 25, 2023

https://data.unhcr.org/en/documents/details/98334

Weinbaum, Marvin, “The Taliban’s two-track strategy,” Middle East Institute, June 8, 2020.

“White House shifts Afghanistan strategy towards talks with Taliban,” Guardian, July 19, 2010.

"Who are the Taliban?," BBC, 12 August 2022

https://www.bbc.com/news/world-south-asia-11451718

“Who Will Run the Taliban Government?” International Crisis Group, September 9, 2021.

Yousaf, Kamran, "Why is India embracing the Afghan Taliban?" The Express Tribune, June 06, 2022

https://tribune.com.pk/story/2360222/why-is-india-embracing-the-afghan-taliban

Younus, Uzair, Ahmed, Roohan, "With No Help from Kabul, Pakistan Faces the TTP Threat," New Lines Institute for Strategy and Policy, January 19, 2023

https://newlinesinstitute.org/pakistan/with-no-help-from-kabul-pakistan-faces-the-ttp-threat/

Yusufzai, Mushtaq, Mengli, Ahmed and Silva, Chantal Da, “From Afghan nation-builder to life in ‘exile’: Ashraf Ghani flees country in defeat,” NBC News, August 16, 2021. https://www.nbcnews.com/news/world/afghan-nationbuilder-life-exile-ashraf-ghani-flees-country-defeat-n1276826

Yousaf, Kamran, "Pakistan, China discuss extending CPEC to Afghanistan," The Express Tribune, July 18, 2022

Tribune,https://tribune.com.pk/story/2366540/pakistan-china-discuss-extending-cpec-to-afghanistan

Zaidi, Syed Muhammad Zulqurnain, "The Assassination of the Prime Minister Liaquat Ali Khan: The Fateful Journey," National Institute of Historical & Cultural Research, p. 3

http://www.nihcr.edu.pk/Latest_English_Journal/4.%20THE%20ASSASSINATION.pdf

"55 percent Pakistanis 'happy' with Taliban takeover of Afghanistan — survey," Arab News, September 14, 2021

https://www.arabnews.pk/node/1928561/pakistan

REACH THE AUTHOR

Email: furqanraja1122@gmail.com

Twitter: https://twitter.com/furqanraja1122

Facebook: https://www.facebook.com/furqanraja1122/

Instagram: https://www.instagram.com/furqanraja1122/

Printed and Bound by ***Passive Printers*** - www.passiveprinters.com
Printing press that offers Print on Demand (POD) Facility.
Printed in The Islamic Republic of Pakistan.

www.ingramcontent.com/pod-product-compliance
Lightning Source LLC
LaVergne TN
LVHW010111170826
845678LV00012B/2353
* 9 7 8 9 6 9 7 4 9 2 7 1 8 *